40 LESSONS ON PRAYER FROM
THE PEOPLE OF GOD'S WORD

THE PEOPLE OF PRAYER
JOURNAL

KENNETH KUYKENDALL

The People of Prayer Journal
40 Lessons on Prayer from the People of God's Word
©2020 by Kenneth Kuykendall
Cross Roads Publications
ISBN: 978-0-9978232-9-5

Published by Cross Roads Publications
1391 Braselton Hwy.
Lawrenceville, GA. 30043
www.crossroadspublications.org

Printed and published in the United States of America

To Jesus Christ our Great High Priest.

INTRODUCTION

There is no area in the Christian life that is more assaulted by the enemy, misunderstood by the world, neglected by the believer, and adored by the Father than the prayer closet. This is where faith is born, where grace is experienced, where strength is infused, where power is injected, where truth is illuminated, where petitions are made and where answers are given. This is where the Christian life is either won or lost. It should be no surprise, then, that Satan directs his deadliest and most distracting darts at the child of God who attempts to pray.

Out of all the religious obligations of the disciple of Jesus Christ, prayer is perhaps the most problematic and perplexing.

- Do you struggle to pray?
- Do you feel your petitions are hard-pressed to be heard?
- Does your prayer life seem like an awkward exercise of spiritual gymnastics?
- Do you wrestle with *what* to say and *how* to say it when you pray?

If so, you stand shoulder to shoulder with some of the greatest men and women in history. As challenging as prayer can be, God has given us a host of heavenly prayer warriors in His Word for our spiritual gain. They are the people of prayer. Likewise, we are the people of prayer. Prayer is the *one* qualifying attribute of a true believer, regardless of space, time, continent, or covenant. From Old Testament prophets to New Testament preachers, God's people are historically identified as people of prayer.

It is implied throughout Scripture that true believers pray. They may find it difficult, cumbersome, and even baffling at times…but they pray. They may go through dry, cold, indifferent seasons of supplication…but they pray. They may not have an impressive vocabulary, a theological education, or an extensive amount of Bible knowledge…but they pray.

Look around, you will find them gathered at flaming altars where sacrifices are being made unto the Lord. You will find them bowing their hearts to God in tents, tabernacles, and temples. You will find them kneeling in the deserts, standing on the mountains, crying out in the waters deep, and wrestling in the valleys low. And when you find them, you will find them in their prayer closets seeking the face, the will, and the almighty power of God.

Their prayer lives have been given for our example.

I have read countless books on prayer throughout my life, but no greater material is provided than that which has been given in the Word of God. Whatever we know about the deep mysteries of prayer, we know through the victories and defeats, the wins and losses, the weaknesses and strengths of God's people.

In the pages ahead, you will discover forty timeless lessons about prayer. Each lesson will highlight an individual from God's Word and the corresponding virtue that is connected with their prayer life. With each devotion, there are:

- Principles to be considered
- Points to be made
- Passages to be read
- Prayers to be offered
- Ponderings to be answered, and
- Petitions to be recorded.

Become a person of prayer by studying the people who made prayer the practice, the passion, and the pursuit of their lives.

-Kenneth Kuykendall

40 DAY NEW TESTAMENT
READING PLAN

☐ Day 1: Matthew 1-7

☐ Day 2: Matthew 8-12

☐ Day 3: Matthew 13-18

☐ Day 4: Matthew 19-24

☐ Day 5: Matthew 25-28

☐ Day 6: Romans 1-8

☐ Day 7: Romans 9-16

☐ Day 8: 1 Corinthians 1-9

☐ Day 9: 1 Corinthians 10-16

☐ Day 10: Mark 1-4

☐ Day 11: Mark 5-8

☐ Day 12: Mark 9-12

☐ Day 13: Mark 13-16

☐ Day 14: 2 Corinthians 1-13

☐ Day 15: Galatians, Philemon

☐ Day 16: Philippians

☐ Day 17: Acts 1-6

☐ Day 18: Acts 7-10

☐ Day 19: Acts 11-16

☐ Day 20: Acts 17-22

☐ Day 21: Acts 23-28

☐ Day 22: Hebrews

☐ Day 23: James

☐ Day 24:1 and 2 Peter

☐ Day 25: 1&2 Timothy, Titus

☐ Day 26: Luke 1-5

☐ Day 27: Luke 6-10

☐ Day 28: Luke 11-15

☐ Day 29: Luke 16-21

☐ Day 30: Luke 22-24

☐ Day 31: Ephesians, Colossians

☐ Day 32: 1&2 Thessalonians

☐ Day 33: John 1-5

☐ Day 34: John 6-10

☐ Day 35: John 11-16

☐ Day 36: John 17-21

☐ Day 37: 1,2,3 John, Jude

☐ Day 38: Revelation 1-7

☐ Day 39: Revelation 8-14

☐ Day 40: Revelation 15-22

CONTENTS

"There is no greater hindrance to secret prayer in all the world than secret sins; therefore stand upon your watchtower, and arm yourselves with all your might against them."

-Thomas Brook

1

THE PRAYER OF

ADAM

HOW SIN HINDERS OUR FELLOWSHIP
WITH GOD IN PRAYER

Date: _____

Such divine and holy praying has never been known as that which was experienced by Adam. The first man, fashioned in God's image, was uniquely separated from all living creatures in that he found joy in his relationship with the Creator. If prayer's ultimate purpose is to abide in the uninterrupted fellowship of God, then Adam had in the beginning of time that which fallen humanity has longed to have throughout the ages: Communion. Adam was the epitome of prayer.

All the earth was praying ground for Adam. Every word from his mouth was a perpetual petition before His Maker. Ceaseless supplication was the heartbeat of his existence. Oh, to know such divine bliss and holy communion! No other soul in history had in prayer what Adam had...and subsequently lost.

God's first recorded question reveals the heartbreak of man's broken communion, "Adam, where art thou?" (Genesis 3:9). It's not that God was clueless of Adam's estate; on the contrary, God knew exactly what happened and sought to clarify in Adam's conscience the reason for this newfound guilt and shame. Adam had previously been clothed in the glory of God's image; but that image, now marred by the destruction of sin, left him naked, fearful, banished from the table of fellowship. Out of all that Adam lost on that dreaded day in history, nothing was more off-putting than what he lost in his prayer life.

Adam's rebellion teaches us an optimal truth about prayer: The only way *to pray* to God is *to live* to God. Sin and righteousness cannot coexist in the prayer closet. The psalmist declared, "If I regard iniquity in my heart, the LORD will not hear me" (Psalm 66:18). The prophet Isaiah said, "But your iniquities have separated between you and your God, and your sins have hid his face from you, that he will not hear" (Isaiah 59:2).

Sin shuts the door to open communion. It chokes out the seed with thorns and thistles. It stains the soul, sours the spirit, stagnates the water, and suppresses the heart. Sin grieves the Holy Ghost, closes the Bible, and dismisses us from faith's household. But as much as sin hinders prayer, be it known, prayer hinders sin!

When God chose to restore Adam, He went back to the prayer closet and picked out coats of skin for him to wear. Through the death of a sinless sacrifice, God invited fallen man to Himself once again, to pull up a seat, and enjoy the riches of His grace. Even so, Christ Jesus has covered our sins. He has not only given us access to a life of prayer but through a life of prayer He has given us access.

PRAYER PRINCIPLE

If there is sin in my life, I will not be able to experience all that God intends my prayer life to be. Repenting of sin is the first step toward a joyful and meaningful life of prayer.

PRAYER POINTS:

- The ultimate purpose of prayer is to experience holy and uninterrupted communion with God.
- The only way to pray to God is to live to God.
- I cannot disassociate my *life* from my *prayer life*, they are one and the same.
- Sin keeps me out of fellowship with God, thus eliminating true joy, fulfillment, and sense of purpose.

PRAYER PASSAGES

- "For there is one God, and one mediator between God and men, the man Christ Jesus;" (1 Timothy 2:15).
- "Draw nigh to God, and he will draw nigh to you. Cleanse your hands ye sinners; and purify your hearts, ye double minded" (James 4:8)

PRAYER PETITION

Gracious and Merciful Savior, I confess my sins. I ask forgiveness for my transgressions. Wash me, cleanse me, and make me whole. May I commune with You daily through prayer and meditation. As I enter the prayer closet, may I dismiss myself from the pleasures of this world. May all my life be my prayer life.

PRAYER PONDERINGS:

Try to describe the fellowship Adam had with God in the garden.

_____

_____

_____

_____

_____

How did God restore Adam's fellowship and communion?

_____

_____

_____

_____

Describe the connection that sin and prayerlessness have in your life.

_____

_____

_____

_____

_____

How does Jesus restore our fellowship with God when we sin?

_____

_____

_____

_____

_____

PRAYER PAGE:

What I have learned today about prayer:

_____

_____

_____

_____

_____

Today I am thankful for:

_____

_____

_____

_____

_____

Today I am asking for:

_____

_____

_____

_____

_____

My confession before God today is:

_____

_____

_____

_____

_____

"Prayer helps the consecrated man in maintaining his attitude of consecration, keeps him alive to God, and aids him in doing the work to which he is called into, which he has given himself."

– E.M. Bounds

2

THE PRAYER OF

ABEL

HOW PRAYER IS AN OFFERING OF
OUR LIVES UNTO GOD

Date: _____

Fig leaf theology has never impressed God. Adam's fleshly, self-produced, sewn-together works of righteousness could not satisfy the holy requirements of the Lord. Only bloodshed can impart life to man's depraved soul. Through coats of skin, God covered Adam and set forth an eternal precedent of what it takes to enter His presence. Sacrifice alone is the only grounds upon which sinful man can stand before holy God. This was the new order of fallen paradise. Adam and his sons could only gain access to God through prayer offerings.

Therefore, you can image how offensive it must have been when Cain presented to God what God refused from Cain's father: The works of self-righteousness. The "fruit of the ground" that was offered by Cain was no different than the fig-leaf aprons of Adam's pride. Cain's offering disregarded the holy ordinance of God, thus displacing himself from true communion and prayer.

In contrast, Abel came before the Lord with an offering of blood, a sacrifice of the highest sort. Scripture tells us that he brought the "firstlings of his flock and of the fat thereof. And the LORD had respect unto Abel and his offering" (Genesis 4:4). Abel's prayer was pleasing unto God because it was offered on God's terms, not in self-righteousness, but in sacrifice. Such an offering is still the standard for any believer who longs to pray.

Prayer requires death. Prayer is received by the One Who willingly died to be a faithful High Priest; and prayer must be offered by those who daily die to self. It is not just praise that God is looking for, it is the "sacrifice of praise" that is well-pleasing in His sight (Hebrews 13:15).

Therefore, we must take that which we love in the flesh, our "firstlings and the fat thereof" and slaughter it before the Lord. This is prayer. This the mighty upswing of the soul toward heaven. No man can truly pray until he slits the throat of any desire, any aspiration, that could potentially take the place of God.

Many well-meaning and gifted men have sought to please God in the order of Cain, but their prayers go unheard because they fail to sacrifice their time, their mornings, their habits, their affections, their careers, their aspirations, and their indulgences to the Lord. With self-righteousness they try to gain His hear. They speak much but God is never honored in their petitions. Instead, He waits for the offering of Abel. There, on the stained ground of sacrifice, God promises to meet us, to hear us, to commune with us, and to be pleased with the only acceptable form of prayer: The kind that is offered by the giving of our lives.

PRAYER PRINCIPLE

God is pleased in our praying when we offer the entirety of our lives to Him as a sacrifice. Prayer, at that point, becomes an act of full submission to His will.

PRAYER POINTS:

- What we bring to God in prayer determines our view of His Word and His character.
- When we approach God in prayer, we must come before Him on the merit of Christ's sacrifice.
- The prayers of the self-righteous can never please God.
- The man who dies to his own desires will inevitably experience the joy of living in God's presence.

PRAYER PASSAGES

- "I beseech you therefore, brethren, by the mercies of God, that ye present your bodies a living sacrifice, holy, acceptable unto God which is your reasonable service" (Romans 12:1).
- "For by him therefore let us offer the sacrifice of praise to God continually, that is, the fruit of our lips giving thanks to his name" (Hebrews 13:15).

PRAYER PETITION

Faithful Father, May I bring before You my absolute best. Help me to enter my prayer closet with the sacrifice of praise and the giving of my heart to You. Be pleased in my offering as I bow all my life at Your feet.

PRAYER PONDERINGS:

Do you relate more to the prayers of Cain or Abel?

_____

_____

_____

_____

_____

What does the statement "Prayer requires death" mean to you?

_____

_____

_____

_____

_____

Why do you think mankind is reluctant to give his best to God?

_____

_____

_____

_____

_____

How do you offer the sacrifice of praise in terms of praying?

_____

_____

_____

_____

_____

PRAYER PAGE:

What I have learned today about prayer:

_____

_____

_____

_____

_____

Today I am thankful for:

_____

_____

_____

_____

_____

Today I am asking for:

_____

_____

_____

_____

_____

My confession before God today is:

_____

_____

_____

_____

_____

"The great people of the earth today are the people who pray. I do not mean those who talk about prayer; nor those who say they believe in prayer; nor yet those who can explain about prayer; but I mean these people who take time and pray."

– S.D. Gordon

3

THE PRAYER OF

ENOCH

HOW BEING WITH GOD
IS THE GREATEST REWARD OF PRAYER

Date: _____

The benefits and blessings of prayer are as wide, and deep, and long, and high as the God to whom we pray. If God is able to do "exceeding abundantly above all that we ask or think," then we must surmise there is no limitation to what can be accomplished through prayer. Spurgeon said,

> "Prayer is always the preface of blessing. It goes before the blessing as the blessing's shadow. When the sunlight of God's mercies rises upon our necessities, it casts shadow of prayer far down upon the plain."

Prayer is not only the preface of blessing that casts forth a shadow; I would contend that prayer is the very face of blessing itself. How often I have felt despondent of soul, weary in well-doing, beggarly in spirit, only to find myself enraptured anew in the hour of prayer. Such times do not always provide answers to questions or remedies to problems; instead, they supply me with something far greater, something far more needed: The soulful pleasure of simply being with God. The great reward of prayer is not walking away with some sought-after possession in hand; no, the great reward of prayer is simply walking away with God.

Such is the testimony of Enoch's prayer life.

Enoch lived just seven generations after Adam's fall. Humanity had not only grown in number; it had grown in wickedness. God saw that man's heart was evil continually, walking to the course of his own desires. One man, however, chose a different path.

The writer of Hebrews said of Enoch that "he had this testimony, that he pleased God." Subsequently the writer said, "for he that cometh to God must believe that he is, and that he is a rewarder of them that diligently seek him (Hebrews 11:5-6).

This great synopsis of Enoch's faith proved two things about his prayer life: 1). Enoch came to God, diligently seeking Him by prayer and faith, and 2). Enoch was rewarded through his prayer efforts. Literally, Enoch's prayer life was out of this world. One day Enoch was walking and talking with God on earth, then suddenly, Enoch was walking and talking with God in heaven.

Those who have experienced the presence of God in prayer, often confess the same experience. "In the body or out of the body," I cannot tell. Heaven abounds in me, and I seem to abound in heaven. I am in Christ and He is in me making me known to the Father and making the Father known to me.

God being pleased with our praying will never be a possibility if He is not first pleased with our lives. When we walk with God in prayer, we will be able to talk to God in power.

PRAYER PRINCIPLE

When prayer is reduced to a list of items that we need from heaven's supply chain, we miss the whole point of prayer. The greatest reward of prayer is being with God in holy communion.

PRAYER POINTS:

- Prayer is the practice of walking with God.
- Though God desires to bless me with answers in prayer, nothing in prayer is greater than God Himself.
- It is possible to walk in holy communion with God even in a depraved, evil, wicked society.
- Pleasing the Lord in my prayer life is the result of living for God in every area of life.

PRAYER PASSAGES

- "If we live in the Spirit, let us also walk in the Spirit" (Galatians 5:25)
- "For we are his workmanship, created in Christ Jesus unto good works, which God hath before ordained that we should walk in them" (Ephesians 2:10).

PRAYER PETITION

Holy God, The desire of my heart is to be thrilled by Your glorious presence. As I submit my soul to You, let me walk in holiness, purity, and love. May the pursuit of my prayers be nothing less than You. Oh, to know You, to hear You, to see Your glory! Fashion my steps to follow You all the days of my life.

PRAYER PONDERINGS:

Give five words that detail God's presence in the moment of prayer.

_____

_____

_____

_____

_____

How does your walk outside of the prayer closet affect your prayers?

_____

_____

_____

_____

_____

On a scale from 1 to 10, measure the intimacy you have with God.

_____

_____

_____

_____

_____

Would others consider you to be a man or woman of prayer?

_____

_____

_____

_____

_____

PRAYER PAGE:

What I have learned today about prayer:

_____

_____

_____

_____

_____

Today I am thankful for:

_____

_____

_____

_____

_____

Today I am asking for:

_____

_____

_____

_____

_____

My confession before God today is:

_____

_____

_____

_____

_____

"Our lives should be, according to our Lord's plans, quiet but steadily flowing streams of blessing, which through our prayers and intercessions should reach our whole environment."

– Ole Hallesby

4

THE PRAYER OF

NOAH

HOW PRAYER CAN INFLUENCE
OTHERS FOR GENERATIONS TO COME

Date: _____

Noah was a builder. He built a reputation of righteousness. He built a family who loved God. He built an ark to the saving of his household. He built a civilization after a world-wide flood. And he built an altar of prayer as an act of worship and thanksgiving. As a matter of fact, Noah was the first man in Scripture, perhaps history, who built an altar to God.

In the post-flood world, Noah sought not shelter, food, or water. Rather, he sought a designated place to glorify God and lead his family in prayer. Eight souls, the entirety of humanity, stood around the altar and watched as Noah offered burnt offerings before the Lord. The sweet-smelling savor of Noah's prayer pleased the Lord in such a way that He promised not to "curse the ground anymore" and sealed the promise by putting a bow in the clouds. "God blessed Noah and his sons, and said unto them, Be fruitful, and multiply, and replenish the earth" (Genesis 9:1).

The perpetuity of prayer is an amazing thing. Prayer can be made in the milliseconds of a moment, and yet live on for years, decades, and even generations to come. E.M Bounds said:

> "God shaped the world by prayer. Prayers are deathless. The lives that uttered them may be closed in death, the heart that filled them have ceased to beat, but the prayers lived before God and God's heart is set on them and prayers outlive the lives of those who uttered them; they outlive a generation, outlive an ancient, outlive a world."

It is impossible to know the far-reaching and long-lasting effects of prayer. Noah had no idea how his offering would set forth a divine precedent of sacrifice. He not only constructed an altar for his family, he established a pattern of prayer for patriarchs yet to come. The many altars of Abraham, Moses, and Joshua can be traced back to Noah's prayer life. The altar in the temple was designated as a place, like Noah's altar, to meet God. Noah may have said "amen" to his prayer, but the truth is, his prayer lived on. It lived on in the lives of his sons, and his grandchildren, and in every passing generation. God multiplied them, made them fruitful, and replenished the earth through the prayer of one man.

Such promise there is when you and I offer our prayers to God! If we were to see the permanence that exists in the petitions of prayer, we would be more exact and precise in our offerings. Prayer has an audience with the timeless One. Prayer is placed before the heavenly altar where there are no bounds or limitation. So, when we pray, we operate beyond our own time, strength, and ability. God breathes upon such prayers and His breath is eternal.

PRAYER PRINCIPLE

Our prayer lives can influence others long after we are gone. They are not bound by our limitations but can function and operate in the eternal Spirit of our God, thus impacting generations to come.

PRAYER POINTS:

- God is well pleased when I offer sacrifices of praise.
- The greatest influence I can have on my family is to build in their conscience the need and desire of prayer.
- Long after I have made an end of supplication, prayer has the unique power to live beyond my words.
- God can use my prayer life to establish a pattern of prayer in the lives of others.

PRAYER PASSAGES

- "I will wash my hands in innocency: so will I compass thine altar, O LORD:" (Psalm 26:6).
- "I beseech you, brethren, (ye know the house of Stephanas, that it is the firstfruits of Achaia. and that they have addicted themselves to the ministry of the saints)" (1 Corinthians 16:15).

PRAYER PETITION

Almighty God, It is unfathomable to me how You can take my prayer and use it beyond my own life. What power there is in holy petition! What glory there is in Your strength and might. As I pray, create in others a desire to know You, to do Your will. Let my life be an altar for others.

PRAYER PONDERINGS:

How often do you pray with your family?

_____
_____
_____
_____
_____

How have you been impacted by the prayers of others before you?

_____
_____
_____
_____
_____

In what ways would you like for God to use your prayer life?

_____
_____
_____
_____
_____

Do you agree with E.M. Bounds statement, "Prayers are deathless"?

_____
_____
_____
_____
_____

PRAYER PAGE:

What I have learned today about prayer:

_____

_____

_____

_____

_____

Today I am thankful for:

_____

_____

_____

_____

_____

Today I am asking for:

_____

_____

_____

_____

_____

My confession before God today is:

_____

_____

_____

_____

_____

"Faith is to the soul what life is to the body. Prayer is to faith what breath is to life. How a man can live and not breathe is past my comprehension, and how a man can believe and not pray is past my comprehension too."

– J.C. Ryle

5

THE PRAYER OF

ABRAHAM

HOW FAITH ESTABLISHES PRAYER,
AND HOW PRAYER ESTABLISHES FAITH

Date: _____

Faith and prayer are mutually dependent on each other in that they both have God as their object. Prayer requires faith in God. How else can we pray to a God we have not seen? If we are to come to the Lord in prayer, we must "believe that he is, and that he is a rewarder of them that diligently seek him" (Hebrews 11:6). Without faith, our prayers are no different than the half-crazed imbeciles who talk to themselves in random fashion.

Not only does prayer require faith in God, but simultaneously, faith in God requires prayer. As God is the object of faith, He is equally the object of prayer. Prayer is what unleashes faith. Prayer helps me obtain the promises of God. Prayer sustains my soul. It enables my spirit to ask God for the things that I ought to ask Him for. Prayer helps me to facilitate "things hoped for, the evidence of things not seen." I need faith *and* I need prayer; *and* I need them both working together at the same time.

Abraham embodied praying faith and faith-filled praying. He went nowhere without these two companions. By faith, he obeyed the heavenly command to receive an inheritance. By faith he sojourned in the land of promise. By faith he looked for a city which "hath foundations, whose builder and maker is God." (Hebrews 11:9-10). However, wherever he went by faith, he brought prayer along, "and there be builded an altar unto the LORD and called upon the name of the LORD" (Genesis 12:8). No other man in the Old Testament constructed more prayer altars than Abraham. Strong was this conviction of prayer because he understood, "What things soever ye desire, when ye pray, believe that ye receive them, and ye shall have them" (Mark 11:24).

Prayer is the act of reaching out *to God* to obtain the promises *of God* that can only be received by faith *in God.* Prayer answers the question of faith, "Believe ye that I am able to do this?" In divine fashion, God almost always responds, "In accordance to your faith." (Matthew 9:28-29).

If you want to know the measure of your faith, evaluate the condition of your prayer life. Cold, impervious praying has never propelled any soul into the realm of believe. It is only in desperate praying that a man can cry out by faith, "I beseech thee, shew me thy glory." When we draw nigh to God on praying ground, He will increase our faith through answered prayers and cause us to pray with unshakable faith. It is then He does "beyond what we can ask or think" because that is when faith implores praying and God is in the business of hearing and answering our prayers.

PRAYER PRINCIPLE

To pray without faith is an impossibility and to have faith without prayer is an impracticality. Prayer is faith in action and faith is prayer in attitude, both intertwined with God as its primary objective.

PRAYER POINTS:

- I cannot pray to God without having faith in God.
- In faith, I pray believing that God will hear me and answer my request.
- Both my prayers and my faith can increase when I live unto God with sincerity of heart.
- God delights in answering my prayers because He is a rewarder of them who diligently seeks Him.

PRAYER PASSAGES

- "And he believed in the LORD; and he counted it to him for righteousness" (Genesis 15:6).
- "Now the just shall live by faith: but if any man draw back, my soul shall have no pleasure in him" (Hebrews 10:38).

PRAYER PETITION

Heavenly Father, It is with a believing heart that I come to You in prayer. I know You are able to do exceeding abundantly beyond what I ask or think. Give me faith to pray and give me the kind of prayers that exercise my faith in Your promises. By faith I call to you and trust in You.

PRAYER PONDERINGS:

What are you specifically asking God for in your prayers?

_____

_____

_____

_____

_____

Describe the relationship of prayer and faith.

_____

_____

_____

_____

_____

Do you believe God prompts you to ask for things when you pray?

_____

_____

_____

_____

_____

Based upon your prayer life, how would you measure your faith?

_____

_____

_____

_____

_____

PRAYER PAGE:

What I have learned today about prayer:

_____

_____

_____

_____

_____

Today I am thankful for:

_____

_____

_____

_____

_____

Today I am asking for:

_____

_____

_____

_____

_____

My confession before God today is:

_____

_____

_____

_____

_____

"The assurance of answered prayers comes from Him, and He it is that makes prayer the mightiest force in the universe of God. The secret of it all is in Him. The power of it all is by Him. The joy of it all is with Him."
— Samuel Chadwick

6

THE PRAYER OF

HAGAR

HOW PRAYER GAINS THE EAR OF GOD
IN TIMES OF HOPELESSNESS AND DESPERATION

Date: _____

What sounds like a modern-day saga of an abandoned pregnant teenage girl is actually the age-old story of Sarah's handmaid Hagar. Impatient with the divine promise of having a child, Sarah took matters into her own hands and convinced Abraham to have marital relations with Hagar. When she became pregnant, animosity grew so strongly between the matriarch and her servant girl that Hagar fled from Sarah's indignation. Pregnant, despised, homeless, and exiled in the wilderness, Hagar was all alone...or so she thought.

In her utter despair, the Lord heard her cry. He found her near a fountain in the region of Shur and began enquiring of her situation. "Why are you here? "Where will you go?" After she poured her heart out to the Lord, He comforted her, and told her to go back home with the promise of a child, "Thou shalt call him Ishmael; because the LORD hath heard thy affliction" (Genesis 16:11).

With divine solace, Hagar cried out to God in prayer. She called His name El Roi, "the God Who sees me" and said, "Have I also here looked after Him that seeth me?" (Genesis 16:13).

Hagar teaches us many things about prayer, but perhaps nothing greater than this: Desperation gains the ear of God.

The sensitivity of God's heart is mightier than a mother's instinct or a father's arm. He inclines Himself toward our poverty. He leans in the direction of our loneliness. He muses over our misery and moves any mountain to make His mercy known. In such grace, He oftentimes prompts the very prayer that we need to pray. We know not what to ask for lest He direct our hearts to the asking. We know not what to seek after lest He reveal in our spirit what must be sought. We know not what door to knock upon, lest He open it before us in our presence. Nothing is more distilling to the overwhelmed heart than to know that God interprets, dissects, and understands the language of sorrow. To the praying saint, there is something heavenly about helplessness.

When we pray in this manner, God finds us, God speaks to us, and God prays for us before the throne. It is there the abandoned can feel welcomed, the dejected can know love, the exiled can find refuge, and those who are barren with sorrow become pregnant with the promise of hope.

One may look upon Hagar with pity and shame, but the truth is, anyone who wants to be heard of God must come with the same quality and condition of heart. For such is our confidence, "The LORD is nigh unto them that are of a broken heart; and saveth such as be of a contrite spirit" (Psalm 34:18).

PRAYER PRINCIPLE

God is drawn toward desperation. When we are troubled and overwhelmed with a heart full of angst, He not only sees us and hears us, He prompts us to pray and prays on our behalf.

PRAYER POINTS:

- God understands every emotion of the heart.
- God oftentimes uses adverse situations to ignite prayer in our lives.
- God not only sees our desperation; He speaks to us and provides answers for our dilemmas.
- When we do not know what to do, or what to pray for, God illuminates through prayer what needs to be done.

PRAYER PASSAGES

- "For in the time of trouble he shall hide me in his pavilion: in the secret of his tabernacle shall he hide me; he shall set me up upon a rock" (Psalm 27:5).
- "Humble yourselves therefore under the mighty hand of God, that he may exalt you in due time: Casting all your care upon him; for he careth for you" (1 Peter 5:6-7).

PRAYER PETITION

Mighty Savior and Deliverer, I come before You with a broken heart, and a contrite spirit. Hear and see me in my despair. Shine Your light upon me and give hope to my soul. When I feel abandoned, tired, and weary, remind me that You see me and hear my cry.

PRAYER PONDERINGS:

Do you sense more of God's presence in times of sorrow? If so, why?

_____

_____

_____

_____

_____

Do you believe God reveals to us what we ought to pray?

_____

_____

_____

_____

_____

What does the name *El Roi* mean to you personally?

_____

_____

_____

_____

_____

How does desperation improve praying? Are you desperate?

_____

_____

_____

_____

_____

PRAYER PAGE:

What I have learned today about prayer:

_____
_____
_____
_____
_____

Today I am thankful for:

_____
_____
_____
_____
_____

Today I am asking for:

_____
_____
_____
_____
_____

My confession before God today is:

_____
_____
_____
_____
_____

"The event certainly has been decided – in a sense it was decided 'before all worlds.' But one of the things taken into account in deciding it, and therefore one of the things that really cause it to happen, may be this very prayer that we are now offering."

– C.S. Lewis

7

THE PRAYER OF

ELIEZER

HOW PRAYING SPECIFIC PRAYERS
GIVES WAY TO SPECIFIC ANSWERS

Date: _____

E liezer, the servant of Abraham, was given the monumental task of finding a bride for the promised son, Isaac. This was no small assignment; it would be through the seed of Isaac that all the nations of the world would be blessed. The messianic implication of this historic mission was one of great responsibility, one that laid heavily upon the servant. He was not called upon to simply pick out any lady to his liking; no, he knew his selection must be ordained of God. Therefore, when we came to Mesopotamia, just outside of Nahor, he stopped by a well and made this prayer unto the Lord:

> "O LORD God of my master Abraham, I pray thee, send me good speed this day, and show kindness unto my master Abraham. Behold I stand here by the well of water; and the daughters of the men of the city come out to draw water: And let it come to pass, that the damsel to whom I shall say, Let down thy pitcher, I pray thee, that I may drink; and she shall

say, Drink, and I will give thy camels drink also: let the same be she that thou has appointed for thy servant Isaac; and thereby shall I know that thou hast showed kindness unto my master" (Genesis 24:12-14).

Eliezer prayed that the appointed "damsel" would not only offer him something to drink but would provide water for his entourage of camels. Before he could finish praying, Rebekah approached the well and offered water to Eliezer in the exact fashion in which he prayed. God not only gave an immediate answer, He gave an answer in response to the specifications of the prayer.

Specific praying yields specific results. What kind of father would provide a serpent when his child asks for a fish? Who would give their son a plate of stones when the request was for bread? I suppose serpents and stones have their benefit in different settings, but the father gives in accordance with the request. Therefore, fish and bread are given by the father because that is what was asked for by the children.

And so it is with our heavenly Father. If we have not, it is because we have failed to ask; or if we have asked, it so generic and broad that God's glory would be concealed in the giving. Eliezer's request was so specific that only God could have answered it, and only God could have received worship in the answering. God loves bestowing gifts in this manner. It is in the smallest detail that God works his greatest miracles. Therefore, let us put away vague generalities, away with vain repetition. Good gifts, certain gifts, specific gifts remain for His children. He is waiting on you even now to make your requests known.

PRAYER PRINCIPLE

It is specific praying that yields specific results. God works in the details of our requests so that when He answers there will be no mistake as to Who should receive the glory.

PRAYER POINTS:

- As God's children, we are invited to let our requests be made known unto God.
- Generalizations in praying require little faith.
- It is the good pleasure of our Father to bestow specific answers for specific needs.
- God receives optimal glory in specific prayers because such praying requires an ability beyond man's strength.

PRAYER PASSAGES

- "And Jesus stood still, and called them, and said, What will ye that I shall do unto you? They say unto him, Lord, that our eyes may be opened...and immediately their eyes received sight, and they follow him" (Matthew 20:32-34).
- "And whatsoever ye shall ask in my name, that will I do, that the Father may be glorified in the Son" (John 14:13).

PRAYER PETITION

Good and Bountiful Father, Too often I pray with vagueness of heart. I ask that You give me knowledge to know what I should pray for. Help me to fashion my prayers in such a way that when You answer them there will be no denying You the glory and the honor. Amen.

PRAYER PONDERINGS:

Why do you think we often pray in generalities?

_____

_____

_____

_____

_____

What specific needs or requests do you have right now in your life?

_____

_____

_____

_____

_____

How does God receive glory in answering specific prayers?

_____

_____

_____

_____

_____

Do you think that God denies specific requests? Why or why not?

_____

_____

_____

_____

_____

PRAYER PAGE:

What I have learned today about prayer:

_____

_____

_____

_____

_____

Today I am thankful for:

_____

_____

_____

_____

Today I am asking for:

_____

_____

_____

_____

My confession before God today is:

_____

_____

_____

_____

*"One of the most subtle burdens God ever puts
on us as saints is this burden of discernment concerning
other souls. He reveals things in order that we may take
the burden of these souls before Him and form the mind
of Christ about them. It is not that we bring God into
touch with our minds, but that we rouse ourselves until
God is able to convey His mind to us about
the one for whom we intercede."*

– Oswald Chambers

8

THE PRAYER OF

ISAAC

HOW GOD USES PRAYER TO MEET THE
NEEDS OF YOUR COMPANION AND LOVED ONES

Date: _____

Isaac was the son of promise, the heir of faith, the chosen seed of Abraham, the elect of God. All the nations of the earth, past and present, can trace their redemptive blessings back to the lineage of this godly patriarch. So special was Isaac's place in history that when God chose to reveal His name to the children of Israel, He called Himself, "The God of Abraham, the God of Isaac, and the God of Jacob" (Exodos 3:14, Acts 7:32).

Oddly enough, there are only a few occasions of Isaac praying in Scripture, the first being an intercessory prayer for his wife. Though short and pithy in length, it unleashes a powerful lesson of intercession that reaches forth to millenniums to come:

> "And Isaac was forty years old when he took Rebekah to wife...And Isaac entreated the LORD for his wife, because she was barren: and the LORD entreated of him, and Rebekah his wife conceived" (Genesis 25:20-21)

As a child that came forth from a barren womb, Isaac was no stranger of sterile situations. However, unlike his mother, he did not try to manufacture the promise of God through the manipulation of circumstance. Instead, he entreated the Lord through intercessory prayer and positioned his family to receive God's blessings. Isaac's prayer teaches us three lessons.

Intercessory prayer requires love. Charles Spurgeon said, "Earnest intercession will be sure to bring love with it." This is especially true in marriage. We are to love and honor one another so that our "prayers be not hindered" (1 Peter 3:7). Nothing demonstrates Calvary's love more than when we intercede for our barren bride. Such "earnest intercession" will endure the affliction of prayer because it knows that God will meet the need of the one we are praying for.

Intercessory prayer involves longevity. In one solitary verse we find that Isaac prayed for Rebekah; but the context of that verse reveals he prayed that prayer for twenty years. He agonized with God, he continued, he persevered in praying. He "entreated the LORD" on her behalf. He did not give in until God worked a miracle of some kind; intercessory prayer never does. It continues, it presses on, it lays hold of the altar until the blessing comes.

Intercessory prayer produces life. When Isaac entreated the LORD for Rebekah, the LORD in return entreated Isaac; and with double blessing did God honor such prayer. Two nations in the womb of Rebekah is the eternal testimony of God's answer to Isaac's intercession. Be it known: When we pray for others, we release heaven's treasury in their bosom.

PRAYER PRINCIPLE

When God reveals a need that may exist in my spouse's life, it is my call to prayer. No greater act of kindness can be extended toward them than when I spend time supplicating on their behalf.

PRAYER POINTS:

- At the heart of any relationship is the need to pray for those we love.
- Intercessory prayer requires patience and faith as the answer may not come right away.
- When we earnestly entreat for others, God will faithfully entreat with us, thus a double-blessing is obtained.
- God is pleased and honored when we pray for others.

PRAYER PASSAGES

- "Bear ye one another's burdens, and so fulfill the law of Christ" (Galatians 6:2).
- "Husbands, love your wives, even as Christ also loved the church, and gave himself for it;" (Ephesians 5:25).

PRAYER PETITION

Heavenly Father, In Your name I bring the needs of my spouse, my children, my loved ones, and my friends to You. I ask that You strengthen them with might in the inner man. Fill them with the fullness of God. Give them the ability to comprehend the love of Christ. Keep them safe, guide their feet, and pour out Your blessings upon their lives. Amen.

PRAYER PONDERINGS:

What specific needs does your spouse currently have?

_____

_____

_____

_____

_____

Do you and your companion spend time together in prayer?

_____

_____

_____

_____

_____

Is there anything you have been praying about for a long time?

_____

_____

_____

_____

_____

How does God bless the intercessor when he/she prays for others?

_____

_____

_____

_____

_____

PRAYER PAGE:

What I have learned today about prayer:

_____
_____
_____
_____
_____

Today I am thankful for:

_____
_____
_____
_____

Today I am asking for:

_____
_____
_____
_____

My confession before God today is:

_____
_____
_____
_____

"*Prayer is not merely the meeting of two moods or two affections, the laying of the head on a divine bosom in trust and surrender. That may have its place in religion, but it is not the nerve and soul of prayer. Nor is it religious reverie. Prayer is an encounter of wills – till one will or the other give way.*"

– P.T. Forsyth

9

THE PRAYER OF

JACOB

HOW WRESTLING WITH GOD IN
PRAYER PRODUCES A CHANGED LIFE

Date: _____

Nothing is more tempestuous about prayer than it being a battle of the wills. Jacob, known for his mischievous and conniving ways fashioned his will against others in a self-preserving, self-aggrandizing manner. He deceived his father Isaac, he usurped his brother Esau, and he manipulated his father-in-law Laban. Known as the supplanter, the deceiver, the great trickster of the Old Testament, he was as strong-willed as any patriarch in history. If wit and strength were the contest, Jacob had no contenders. The fact that he never backed down from a fight brought many a curse to his life; ironically enough, it also brought divine blessing.

One night in the region of Jabbok, Jacob locked arms with deity, he grabbed hold of heaven, he wrestled with a warrior from another world. Not for one measly round, but the entire night Jacob struggled with God in a battle of the wills. His birthright was secure, his possessions were many, his estate was large, but his relationships were maligned, his conscience was heavy, and his guilt was unrelenting. And so, he wrestled, he fought, he refused to let go until something changed in his life. Though he was no match for the holy One of heaven, Jacob refused defeat. With resolved tone, he cried out to God, "I will not let you go, except thou bless me" (Genesis 32:26). At that moment, God changed Jacob's name to Israel, "for as a prince hast thou power with God and with men, and hast prevailed" (Genesis 32:28).

God not only changed Jacob's name, He changed his heart, his life, and his witness throughout all the world. Such is the power of persevering prayer. In the book, *The Soul of Prayer*, P.T. Forsyth says that wrestling with God is really the dominant idea of prayer:

> "Prayer is not merely the meeting of two moods or two affections, the laying of the head on a divine bosom in trust and surrender. That may have its place in religion, but it is not the nerve and soul of prayer. Nor is it religious reverie. Prayer is an encounter of wills...till one will or the other give way."

Prayer ground is battle ground. When we determine to lay hold of God in prayer and refuse to let go until the blessing comes, it is then, and only then, we position ourselves for divine benevolence. It is then we lay claim to providence. It is there, in that holy arena that we long for God to interfere with our affairs, to intercede on our behalf. And though our thigh be out of joint, and though we limp like Jacob the rest of our days, we will have known the joy of winning the battle. For it is after the wrestling, God provides the rest. And be sure, we will need it after such holy contest.

PRAYER PRINCIPLE

To wrestle with God in prayer means to persevere, to endure, to refuse life without His interference and assistance. This kind of praying does not always change our circumstances, but it always changes us.

PRAYER POINTS:

- True prayer is always a battle of the will.
- Engagement of the mind, soul, and spirit is necessary when wrestling with God.
- There is often a price that is to be paid for such praying.
- The benefit of persevering prayer is always greater than the sacrifice in that God changes our lives for His glory.

PRAYER PASSAGES

- "Rejoicing in hope; patient in tribulation; continuing instant in prayer" (Romans 12:12).
- "Praying always with all prayer and supplication in the Spirit, and watching thereunto with all perseverance and supplication for all saints;" (Ephesians 6:18).

PRAYER PETITION

Father God, Give me resolve to continue, faith to believe, and strength to stand. With a spirit of endurance, help me to pray with earnest desire and resolved heart. May I pray until I break through. May I hunger for Your blessing in such fervency that I refuse to let go until You bless me.

PRAYER PONDERINGS:

Do you wrestle with God when you pray? In what ways?

_____

_____

_____

_____

_____

Explain what it means to "win" in the battle of prayer?

_____

_____

_____

_____

_____

Give other bible verses that validate the idea of wrestling with God.

_____

_____

_____

_____

_____

If prayer could change anything in your life, what would it be?

_____

_____

_____

_____

_____

PRAYER PAGE:

What I have learned today about prayer:

_____

_____

_____

_____

_____

Today I am thankful for:

_____

_____

_____

_____

Today I am asking for:

_____

_____

_____

_____

My confession before God today is:

_____

_____

_____

_____

"Earnest intercession will be sure to bring love with it. I do not believe you can hate a man for whom you habitually pray. If you dislike any brother Christian, pray for him doubly, not only for his sake, but for your own, that you may be cured of prejudice and saved from all unkind feeling."

– Charles Spurgeon

10

THE PRAYER OF

MOSES

HOW INTERCESSORY PRAYER
CAN BRING DELIVERANCE FOR OTHERS

Date: _____

It would be too difficult a challenge to characterize the prayer life of Moses by one solitary act of supplication. His entire ministry is marked by ongoing and continual prayer. He lived in the spirit of prayer. It can be determined, however, that the overall tone of his praying was that of an intercessor. Moses was faithful to deliver God's people from Egypt, but the bulk of his ministry consisted of him delivering the people of Egypt from God through prayer. At every turn and on every corner, Moses can be seen pleading for mercy on behalf of those whom God put to his care.

When Israel faced a fierce foe in Amalek, Moses carried the rod of God to the mountain and prayed for victory to come. Had it not been for his prayers they would have surely been defeated. When Israel complained over bread, God sent fiery serpents into the camp and would have killed the entire congregation, but Moses pled for mercy anew. When Israel danced around the golden calf, God would have quickly destroyed them in their idolatry, but Moses prayed, and once again, the mighty and merciful pleas of the man of God prevented their destruction. E.M. Bounds comments:

> "No mission was more majestic in purpose and results than that of Moses, and none was more responsible, diligent and difficult. In it we are taught the sublime ministry and rule of prayer. Not only is it the medium of supply and support, but it is a compassionate agency through which the pitying long-suffering of God has an outflow. Prayer is a medium to restrain God's wrath, that mercy might rejoice against judgment.

In providence, God chooses to restrain His wrath against sinners when God's people intercede on their behalf. A clear illustration of this is given in the gospels. A man sick of the palsy was brought to the Lord on his bed by his friends. They fought the crowd, traveled the distance, tore the roof, and lowered their loved one into the home where Christ was teaching. In so doing, Jesus saw intercessory faith and forgave the man of his sins. Christ did for the palsied what He did for Israel, and what He has done throughout the ages: He pardons men instead of punching them.

Israel, as a nation, endured wilderness travels, overcame hunger and thirst, defeated its enemies, persevered in tribulation, and has survived for millenniums because God imparted mercy through the prayers of an intercessor. Nothing emulates the prayers of Christ more than when we plead before a holy God to extend pardon and grace for those who stand in judgment.

PRAYER PRINCIPLE

Through intercessory prayer, we appeal to the mercies of God begging Him to restrain His judgment from those who have transgressed His law. Through such an appeal, God oftentimes refrains His wrath and imparts forgiveness.

PRAYER POINTS:

- God honors the prayers of those who pray for others.
- The soul that has transgressed the Lord desperately needs the prayers of an intercessor.
- In His providence, God, at times, chooses to refrain His hand of judgment against those who deserve wrath.
- The prayer of intercession is the work of our Great High Priest and Mediator Jesus Christ.

PRAYER PASSAGES

- "Then said Jesus, Father, forgive them; for they know not what they do" (Luke 23:34).
- "Wherefore he is able to save them to the uttermost that come unto God by him, seeing he ever liveth to make intercession for them" (Hebrews 7:25).

PRAYER PETITION

Merciful and Gracious Father, You ever live to make intercession for Your people. I pray that Your ministry of intercession will remind me to pray for others. There are those around me who need grace and mercy. Forgive their sins, heal their souls, and give them hearts of repentance.

PRAYER PONDERINGS:

Why does God honor the prayer of the intercessor?

_____

_____

_____

_____

_____

Do you find it difficult to pray for those who live in sin?

_____

_____

_____

_____

_____

What does it mean that Christ "ever liveth to make intercession"?

_____

_____

_____

_____

_____

What benefits and blessings come along with intercessory prayer?

_____

_____

_____

_____

_____

PRAYER PAGE:

What I have learned today about prayer:

_____

_____

_____

_____

_____

Today I am thankful for:

_____

_____

_____

_____

_____

Today I am asking for:

_____

_____

_____

_____

_____

My confession before God today is:

_____

_____

_____

_____

_____

"If added power attends the united prayer of two or three, what mighty triumphs there will be when hundreds of thousands of consistent members of the Church are with one accord day by day making intercession for the extension of Christ's Kingdom."

— John R. Mott

11

THE PRAYER OF

AARON & HUR

HOW PRAYER PARTNERS CAN HELP
US GAIN VICTORY IN THE BATTLES OF LIFE

Date: _____

It didn't take long after their deliverance from Egypt for Israel to understand the difficulty of wilderness living. In addition to the hunger, the thirst, the complaints, and the murmurings, Moses also had to contend with the logistics of leading millions of people out of one nation and into another. Without any military backing, Israel became a prime target for every rogue group in the area. With the spoils of Egypt in their possession, the likelihood of an attack was imminent.

When Israel entered the region of Rephidim, Amalek made his move against God's elect and fought against the weakest and most feeble among them (Deuteronomy 25:17-18). Instead of cutting his losses and moving forward, Moses decided to stay and fight. Joshua, the commanding officer, was sent to the frontlines of the conflict while Moses went to the top of the hill to engage his own battle; as always, Moses planned to intercede for the people of God in prayer. An incredible dynamic occurred as the war raged.

When Moses raised the rod of God toward heaven, Joshua prevailed over Amalek; but whenever Moses let down the rod of God, Amalek prevailed against Joshua.

The strength of Joshua was made possible by the prayers of Moses. But overtime, the hands of Moses grew weary. Amalek was certain to prevail had it not been for the faithful prayer partners who accompanied Moses on the hill.

Aaron and Hur recognized that the weight of the battle was far too great for Moses to all alone. In wisdom and compassion, they advised Moses to sit upon a stone with the rod of God in his hands. Aaron got on one side of Moses and Hur got on the other side. With resolve and determination, they kept his hands steady until Joshua overcome the enemy.

This beautiful illustration of teamwork demonstrates the need we all have for prayer partners. The weak and feeble of Israel needed the strength of Joshua. Joshua needed the prayers of Moses. Moses needed the assistance of Aaron and Hur. When everyone worked together in harmonious fashion, the enemy was destroyed, and victory was shared throughout the camp.

Aaron and Hur never took the rod of God out of Moses' hands, neither did they take the weight off his shoulders; instead, they partnered together to help bear the load. They got under the burden with him and persevered until victory came. This is the purpose of prayer partners. Prayer is battle, and there are some battles we cannot win by ourselves. Having a trusted ally on the frontlines of conflict always proves to be of great benefit to the soul. It is in such sacred union God promises to be in the midst.

PRAYER PRINCIPLE

Having a trusted prayer partner provides strength, stamina, and security during the most heated battles of life. Victory is more readily available when we enlist others to help us pray.

PRAYER POINTS:

- The enemy oftentimes attack the weakest and most vulnerable elements of our lives.
- Some battles and some conflicts are too difficult for us to face all by ourselves.
- The purpose of a prayer partner is to help us bear the burdens of life.
- God works in the beauty and harmony of His people praying together.

PRAYER PASSAGES

- "And if one prevail against him, two shall withstand him; and a threefold cord is not quickly broken" (Ecclesiastes 4:12).
- "For where two or three are gathered together in my name, there am I in the midst of them" (Matthew 18:20).

PRAYER PETITION

Great God and King, I am thankful for those individuals in my life to whom I can entrust my most personal and private prayers. They have often refreshed me and encouraged me to prevail. May You continually join our hearts together until we see Your marvelous works.

PRAYER PONDERINGS:

What qualities and characteristics should a prayer partner have?

_____

_____

_____

_____

_____

Do you have prayer partners? Why or why not?

_____

_____

_____

_____

_____

Explain how God uses the unity of prayer to give victory.

_____

_____

_____

_____

_____

List any past victories you've had as a result of others praying.

_____

_____

_____

_____

_____

PRAYER PAGE:

What I have learned today about prayer:

_____

_____

_____

_____

_____

Today I am thankful for:

_____

_____

_____

_____

Today I am asking for:

_____

_____

_____

_____

My confession before God today is:

_____

_____

_____

_____

"Prayer is the royal power a child of God exercises in heaven on behalf of others and even of the kingdom."

– Andrew Murray

12

THE PRAYER OF

JOSHUA

HOW PRAYER GIVES WAY
FOR GOD TO DO THE IMPOSSIBLE

Date: _____

Prayer is the means by which God puts Himself full force into the affairs of mankind. Prayer sets forth into motion that which would not have occurred had it not been activated by the audacious asking of some saint. Prayer does the impossible because it calls upon the One Who works in such a realm. In response to the disciple's enquiry about who can enter the kingdom of heaven, Jesus said, "With men this is impossible; but with God all things are possible" (Matthew 19:26).

We want to limit the words of Christ to mean "all things are possible" within reason. "All things are possible" if they can be explained and logically resolved in the minds of men. "All things are possible" if it makes sense. But the truth is, there are many aspects of prayer that does not make sense in the natural realm. Furthermore, there are many answers we receive in prayer that cannot be conceivably reconciled in the minds of unbelievers.

Such is the case with Joshua's prayer. After defeating the city of Ai, the children of Israel faced the collective forces of the Amorite army. The Amorites aligned themselves with five other kings in hopes of destroying the advancement of God's people in the land. As Joshua prepared for the worse, the Lord gave victory against the enemy. Empowered with the promises of God, Joshua and his mighty men overcame the Amorite army. In the heat of the battle, Joshua prayed and asked God to make the sun stand still so that he would have enough time to destroy all the enemy in a solitary day. In an awesome display of unparalleled power, God answered his request:

> "So the sun stood still in the midst of heaven, and hasted not
> to do down about a whole day. And there was no day like that
> before it or after it, that the LORD hearkened unto the voice of
> a man: for the LORD fought for Israel" (Joshua 10:13-14).

Such a daring request is bothersome to unbelievers and many believers alike. For in it, there is a measure of faith that cries for divine intervention, a reaching forth to something beyond human capability or understanding. It calls out from the natural realm for an answer that can only be distributed in the supernatural realm.

Prayer gives life to the barren womb. Prayer calls down fire from heaven. Prayer can restore the health of the afflicted and add years to the dying saint. Prayer can pause the orbit of the noonday sun to shine its rays of hope into the most heated parts of the battle. Prayer has the courage to ask God to do that which only God can do. To be certain, with men this is impossible, but with God all things are possible; and such is the power of prayer.

PRAYER PRINCIPLE

Prayer is the request of God to work that which cannot be manufactured or produced by the hands of men. In such praying, we are not asking God to work beyond His will, rather, we are asking Him to work beyond our capabilities.

PRAYER POINTS:

- The limitations of our lives afford us the opportunity to call upon the God Who cannot be limited.
- Our lack of faith can prevent us from asking the Lord for certain things.
- God's power and omnipotence is oftentimes demonstrated in direct proportion to the requests of our prayers.
- The possibility of prayer produces impossible results.

PRAYER PASSAGES

- "Is anything too hard for the LORD?" (Genesis 18:14).
- "If ye had the faith as a grain of mustard seed, ye might say unto this sycamine tree, Be thou plucked up by the root, and be thou planted in the sea; and it should obey you" (Luke 17:6).

PRAYER PETITION

Awesome and Mighty God, I glorify Your name. There are no restrictions or barriers to Your capabilities. I pray that my faith will increase to ask for things above and beyond my strength. Grant my petition by Your power and make Your glory to shine forth as a result.

PRAYER PONDERINGS:

Why do you think it is difficult for us to ascertain God's power?

_____

_____

_____

_____

_____

Do miracles still happen today in this fashion? Why or why not?

_____

_____

_____

_____

_____

Do you think it is possible to limit the works of God by lack of faith?

_____

_____

_____

_____

_____

Has God ever answered a prayer in your life as "the impossible"?

_____

_____

_____

_____

_____

PRAYER PAGE:

What I have learned today about prayer:

_____

_____

_____

_____

_____

Today I am thankful for:

_____

_____

_____

_____

_____

Today I am asking for:

_____

_____

_____

_____

_____

My confession before God today is:

_____

_____

_____

_____

_____

"If we would pray aright, the first thing we should do is to see to it that we really get an audience with God, that we really get into His very presence. Before a word of petition is offered, we should have the definite consciousness that we are talking to God, and should believe that He is listening and is going to grant the thing that we ask of Him."

– R.A. Torrey

13

THE PRAYER OF

GIDEON

HOW PRAYER CAN HELP US
OVERCOME DOUBT AND FEAR

Date: _____

It had been seven long years of extreme poverty. Every Hebrew harvest had been captured and consumed by the hands of the Midianites. Field and flock alike were taken away; and Israel, because of its sin, was left exiled in caves and mountain dens. Surrounded by the enemy on all sides, they had no hope of freedom or escape. Physically impoverished and spiritually indifferent, they prayed to God and in response to their prayers, the Lord sent a prophet. This prophet not only called on Israel to repent but promised them deliverance in the process.

While the prophet visited the people, the Lord visited Gideon, a man who was plagued with doubt and insecurity. Gideon's family was poor in Manasseh, and by his own admission, he was "least in his father's house." Assuring Gideon of his own valor, God assigned this newfound Judge with the responsibility to lead Israel in battle against the Midianites. Though a visit from the divine should have been enough ammunition to charge the enemy with full force, Gideon was overcome with hesitation. As he prepared for battle, he did what so many people are tempted to do in times of uncertainty: He put out a fleece to God. The word "if" may be small in its spelling, but it can handicap our faith once employed in our prayers. This is the way Gideon prayed,

> "And Gideon said to God, *If* thou wilt save Israel by mine hand, *as thou has said*, Behold, I will put a fleece of wool in the floor..." (Judges 6:36-37)

The Lord had already confirmed deliverance by His word, and that should have been enough, but Gideon needed a sign. God, in His patience and providence answered according to Gideon's request and brought a great victory to Israel under his leadership.

To be certain, Gideon's asking for a sign was riddled with doubt; but the one truth we can glean from his prayer is that God is willing to hear and answer our prayers even if they are weak.

Prayer is an open invitation to open our hearts before the Lord, even if they are enamored with hesitation and insecurity. Why would God answer this reluctant request? Because it was just that...a request, and God is in the business of relieving His children of such trepidation. It is true, the man who learns to pray by faith will be less inclined to pray by fleeces; but if that man continues to pray in sincerity, God will rid him of the fleece by answering his prayers. Never again do we see Gideon putting out his fleece to God. Prayer then, even in its most hesitant form can illuminate the weakest of saints to rise in faith.

PRAYER PRINCIPLE

Prayer gives assurance to the doubtful, hope to the insecure, and strength to the feeble-hearted. Prayer leads to better praying because prayer leads to stronger faith.

PRAYER POINTS:

- Prayer and repentance give way to deliverance.
- God sends a voice of hope whenever His people, in sincerity, seek His face.
- When we fail to heed the Word of God, our prayers will be overwhelmed with doubt and hesitation.
- God invites us to bring our doubt to Him so that He can help us live by faith and assurance.

PRAYER PASSAGES

- "If ye abide in me, and my words abide in you, ye shall ask what ye will, and it shall be done unto you." (John 15:7).
- "But let him ask in faith, nothing wavering. For he that wavereth is like a wave of the sea driven with the wind and tossed" (James 1:6).

PRAYER PETITION

Holy God, There are times when my faith wavers and I need assurance. I know I should trust in Your Word and claim Your promises; but if I am honest, in those weak moments, I put out a fleece. Turn my fleece into faith and help me to trust You more and more. Amen.

PRAYER PONDERINGS:

Is it wrong to put a "fleece" before God? Why or why not?

_____

_____

_____

_____

_____

Are you currently dealing with any hesitation or doubt?

_____

_____

_____

_____

_____

In your own experience, how does prayer overcome doubt?

_____

_____

_____

_____

_____

Do you believe that praying leads to better praying? Explain.

_____

_____

_____

_____

_____

PRAYER PAGE:

What I have learned today about prayer:

_____

_____

_____

_____

_____

Today I am thankful for:

_____

_____

_____

_____

Today I am asking for:

_____

_____

_____

_____

My confession before God today is:

_____

_____

_____

_____

"Do not pray for easy lives.
Pray to be stronger men! Do not pray for
tasks equal to your powers. Pray for
powers equal to your tasks."
– Phillip Brooks

14

THE PRAYER OF

SAMSON

HOW PRAYER CAN STRENGTHEN
US DURING LIFE'S WEAKEST MOMENTS

Date: _____

S amson had a supernatural birth, a superman physique, and a super long hairdo. Somehow, in the divine workings of God, all three components of his identity worked together to produce an extremely powerful and extraordinarily unique individual.

Consecrated at birth with the Nazarite vow, Samson never had a razor upon his head. As his hair grew, so did his strength, notorious strength, uncanny strength. With his bare hands, he killed a lion, tearing it into pieces. On one occasion, he killed thirty men by himself in Ashkelon. With the jawbone of an ass, he destroyed one thousand Philistines in a single battle. This Jewish Judge was no joke. God raised up Samson up, filled him with His Spirit, and unleashed him as a deliverer of God's people.

His only weakness was women. In the lap of Delilah, he poured out the secrets of his strength, fell asleep, and woke up a lesser man. In a plot to emasculate him, Delilah cut the locks of his hair, and turned him over to the Philistines. In their custody, they gauged out his eyes and locked him in fetters of brass. On any other occasion, Samson could have easily overpowered his adversaries, but sadly the Lord had withdrawn His power. Indeed, the mighty had fallen! Samson, a giant among men was now fastened between two pillars being played as the fool. Blind, bound, and belittled, he was soon to be sacrificed to their pagan god Dagon. It was then Samson cried out to God in prayer:

> "O, Lord God, remember me, I pray thee, and strengthen me,
> I pray thee, only this once O God, that I may be at once
> avenged of the Philistines for my two eyes" (Judges 16:28).

God heard his prayer, restored his strength, and as a final act of heroism, gave Samson the power to bring down the two pillars. The entire structure collapsed and though Samson died, he died with power, killing more Philistines in his death than in his life.

Prayer brings power to the soul. It emboldens the most feeble-minded and weak-kneed Christian to battle. It strengthens the heart, it stiffens the will, it stirs the spirit. It takes the most wimpish of men and converts them into heavenly warriors.

The enemy fears nothing of a prayerless saint; nothing of our preaching, or singing, or evangelism, nor even our religious piety. But oh! how the weakest believers become agents of authority at the throne of grace. For it is there that sinners are forgiven, the weak are made strong, and victory is for the taking. How immense and intense is the weaponry of prayer! Its force is so fierce that the mightiest of foes fall when the faintest cries are made.

PRAYER PRINCIPLE

Prayer enables, energizes, and emboldens the saint of God with power from on high. It quickens the spirit to do that which cannot be done in the energy of the flesh. It unleashes the ability of God.

PRAYER POINTS:

- It is possible for believers to lose their spiritual strength.
- The pleasures of sin will bind a believer leaving him ineffective and powerless against the enemy.
- The power we have with God is directly related to the desire we have to pray.
- God can manifest His strength in our weakest moments when we sincerely and earnestly call upon His name.

PRAYER PASSAGES

- "This poor man cried, and the LORD heard him, and saved him out of all his troubles" (Psalm 34:6).
- "And he said unto me, My grace is sufficient for thee: for my strength is made perfect in weakness. Most gladly therefore will I rather glory in my infirmities, that the power of Christ may rest upon me" (1 Corinthians 12:9).

PRAYER PETITION

Strong and Mighty God, I thank You for the power of prayer. There have been so many times in my life I would have failed had it not been for Your strength. Guard my heart against sinfulness and keep my mind pure by Your Word. Let me draw power from the time I spend with You.

PRAYER PONDERINGS:

What brings about spiritual weakness in your life?

_____

_____

_____

_____

_____

Discuss the connection between prayerlessness and weakness.

_____

_____

_____

_____

_____

How does God manifest His power when we pray?

_____

_____

_____

_____

_____

Why is spiritual power necessary for the believer?

_____

_____

_____

_____

_____

PRAYER PAGE:

What I have learned today about prayer:

_____

_____

_____

_____

_____

Today I am thankful for:

_____

_____

_____

_____

_____

Today I am asking for:

_____

_____

_____

_____

_____

My confession before God today is:

_____

_____

_____

_____

_____

*It is not the mouth that is the main thing to
be looked at in prayer, but whether the heart is so full of
affection and earnestness in prayer with God that it is
impossible to express their sense and desire; for then man
desires indeed, when his desires are so strong, many and
mighty that all the words, tears, and groans that come
from the heart cannot utter them."*

– John Bunyan

15

THE PRAYER OF

HANNAH

HOW GOD GIVES US THE DESIRES
OF OUR HEARTS WHEN WE PRAY

Date: _____

Tue prayer, the kind that is heard and honored by God, comes from the heart. It is conceived from above and born from within. As a newborn babe that knows no language, it cries for the sincere milk; it makes its case known with tears until it has latched on to its source of blessing. It cannot be confined with human words nor defined by human hearing. True praying is heart praying.

Many poetic and polished prayers have been articulated before men that have never gained an ear in the heavenlies. John Bunyan said, "This is but poor prayer which is only one of words." It is better to pray with the heart and no words than to pray with words and no heart. Such is the prayer of Hannah.

With a bitter soul and a barren womb, she desperately cried out to God with her heart. When Eli, the high priest, saw her praying, he noticed that "only her lips moved, but her voice was not heard."

What seemed like a drunken stupor to the spiritually inept priest, was in reality the prayer language of a desperate soul who longed to be filled with the promises of God. Eli did not understand her prayers, but the High Priest of Heaven grasped every word.

Hannah desired a child, not just any child, but a certain child; it was for "this child" she prayed. Her heart moved beyond religious rhetoric and Jewish jargon, lifting her request to the very throne of grace. God answered her prayers, gave her a man child in Samuel, and subsequently blessed her with five other children.

There is much to learn from the prayer life of Hannah, but nothing greater than how desire directs the course of our prayers and gets the answer it needs from God. Desire lights the fuel of heaven's flame. It is the breath of life within the lungs of the soul. Desire pushes through the earth like the lily in the lowland, it propels the heart of man to the throne of grace like the salmon that swims upstream. It elevates prayer beyond the first, second, and even third heaven to sit with the One Who can disentangle unspoken words with groanings not known to man.

"When we learn to come to God with an intensity of desire that wrings the soul," said R.A. Torrey, "then we will know a power in prayer that most of us do not know now." E.M. Bounds declared, "Desire is an inward longing for something of which we are not possessed, of which we stand in need…something which God has promised, and which may be secured by an earnest supplication." When desire is hot, prayer will burn in the bosom. It is then that God hears with a ready ear and releases in the belly that which has been wrought in the heart. Such praying is beyond words!

PRAYER PRINCIPLE

If the words of our mouth do not coincide with the desires of our heart, then prayer becomes little more than form and fashion. God delights to give us the desires of our heart when they are sincerely whole and wholly sincere.

PRAYER POINTS:

- Prayer that comes from the heart is the kind of praying that gains the attention of God.
- There are some prayers we pray that are not understood by those around us.
- Desire is the catalyst of effectual praying. It helps navigate our prayers toward the throne of grace.
- A man or woman who lives and abides in the will of God will have the kind of desires that please the Lord.

PRAYER PASSAGES

- "For this child I prayed; and the LORD hath given me my petition which I asked of him" (1 Samuel 1:27).
- "Delight thyself also in the LORD; and he shall give thee the desires of thine heart" (Psalm 37:4).

PRAYER PETITION

Dear Lord, With passion and desire I come before Your throne. Though I may not be able to clearly articulate my request, I ask that You look upon my heart, make sense of my wants and needs, and answer my prayer according to Your will; and make Your will my desire. Amen.

PRAYER PONDERINGS:

Have you ever desired something in prayer that was not God's will?

_____

_____

_____

_____

_____

How can you know if your desires coincide with God's purposes?

_____

_____

_____

_____

_____

In your own words, describe what it means to pray with desire.

_____

_____

_____

_____

_____

List five prayers God has answered as a result of earnest praying.

_____

_____

_____

_____

_____

PRAYER PAGE:

What I have learned today about prayer:

_____
_____
_____
_____
_____

Today I am thankful for:

_____
_____
_____
_____
_____

Today I am asking for:

_____
_____
_____
_____
_____

My confession before God today is:

_____
_____
_____
_____
_____

"No man is greater than his prayer life. We have many organizers, but few agonizers; many players and payers, few pray-ers; many singers, few clingers; lots of pastors, few wrestlers; many fears, few tears; much fashion, little passion; many interferers, few intercessors; many writers, but few fighters. Failing here, we fail everywhere."

– Leonard Ravenhill

16

THE PRAYER OF

SAMUEL

HOW PRAYER ENABLES AND
EMPOWERS RIGHTEOUS LEADERSHIP

Date: _____

The prevailing characteristic of Israel during the time of the judges could be summarized as "every man did that which was right in his own eyes" (Judges 17:6, 21:25). The moral fiber of the nation was just as fickle and fluid as the variety of judges that resided over the land. Moral relativism and spiritual apathy ruled the day thus bringing Israel to a place of indifference and idolatry. So pitiful was the religious state of Israel that Eli, the high priest, considered the desperate prayer of Hannah to be a fit of drunkenness. Perhaps he thought this because he saw such debauchery in his own sons, Hophni and Phinehas. So wicked were the "sons of Belial" that God despised their temple service:

> "Wherefore the sin of the young men was very great before the LORD: for the men abhorred the offering of the LORD. But Samuel ministered before the LORD, being a child, girded with a linen ephod" (1 Samuel 2:17-18).

The nation had no priest, no judge, and no prophet to rule on their behalf; but in the quiet corridors of the holy place, God was preparing a young boy to become all three. The sons of Eli were not only disqualified from the temple, they were ultimately destroyed in battle, along with their father, leaving young Samuel as Israel's newfound leader.

How could such a young child occupy three ordained seats of righteousness? How would he be able to minister in the temple, execute ordinances throughout the land, and proclaim the words of God? In short, through the enabling power of prayer!

Samuel had been born on the wings of prayer. His life was conceived in supplication and received with thanksgiving. His abode in the temple was a testimony of Hannah's prayer offering to the Lord. She had desperately prayed for "this child" and oh, what a man child he was!

It should be no surprise then that Samuel fulfilled his multiple leadership roles in Israel through the continual and persistent exercise of prayer. We find him praying often and regularly for revival, renewal, and restoration. Through prayer, Samuel overcame the Philistines, ordained kings, and earnestly interceded for the sins of the people.

The leadership of Samuel fully demonstrates how "the effectual fervent prayer of a righteous man availeth much" (James 5:16). Prayer produces righteous leaders and righteous leaders will always be found on their knees in prayer. Honor is their lot, truth is their course, virtue is their aim, and prayer is their practice. The leader who is wrought with prayer will be crowned with favor.

PRAYER PRINCIPLE

Spiritual leaders are empowered through their willingness to pray. They realize that the greatest position to be obtained in the kingdom of God is the position upon their knees before the Lord.

PRAYER POINTS:

- The prayerless and careless leader produces a culture of spiritual impotence.
- The effectiveness of a leader cannot be measured by his size, strength, or stature, but rather by his supplication.
- God enables the praying man to fulfill all that is set forth before him.
- Spiritual leadership requires spiritual activity, of which none is greater than prayer.

PRAYER PASSAGES

- "Righteousness exalteth a nation: but sin is a reproach to any people" (Proverbs 14:34)
- "When the righteous are in authority, the people rejoice: but when the wicked beareth rule, the people mourn" (Proverbs 29:2).

PRAYER PETITION

Chief Shepherd and Bishop of my Soul, I ask you to lead me as I lead others. Guide my feet by Your truth as others follow my example. It is only through prayer and supplication that I can lead a quiet and peaceable life. Enable me through prayer to live righteously.

PRAYER PONDERINGS:

What leadership roles have been assigned to you?

_____

_____

_____

_____

_____

Does prayer play a vital role in you fulfilling your assignments?

_____

_____

_____

_____

_____

How does lack of prayer disqualify a man or woman from service?

_____

_____

_____

_____

_____

Cite a few examples of how prayer has empowered your leadership.

_____

_____

_____

_____

_____

PRAYER PAGE:

What I have learned today about prayer:

_____
_____
_____
_____
_____

Today I am thankful for:

_____
_____
_____
_____
_____

Today I am asking for:

_____
_____
_____
_____
_____

My confession before God today is:

_____
_____
_____
_____
_____

*"He who has learned
to pray has learned the secret to
a holy and happy life."*
– William Law

17

THE PRAYER OF

DAVID

HOW PRAYER CREATES
A LIFE OF DEVOTION TO GOD

Date: _____

It is one thing to be a man who prays, it is something altogether different to be a praying man. A man who prays will find certain occasion to bow before God making his requests known to the Lord. A praying man, however, lives before God in the ceaseless and uninterrupted spirit of prayer. A man who prays may *desire something* from the Lord, but the praying man *desires only* the Lord. He longs to be in fellowship with God and desperately pursues Him like a thirsty deer panting after water brooks.

King Saul was a man who prayed. And though he prayed, he lived unto himself with a rebellious and disobedient spirit. He was chosen by the people but had never been ordained of God. His prayers were seldom and random in Scripture, and so was his spiritual influence. In stark contrast was David. David was not only a man who prayed...he was a praying man. He was a praying man because he was a man who pursued the very heart of God.

This is the essence of devotion. God never intends prayer to be a solitary moment among all other events of the day. Such praying will inevitably find itself on a to-do list among a myriad of other menial tasks. Instead, prayer must be the heartbeat of each passing moment until a spirit of prayer is formed in the soul. Prayer was not part of David's life; prayer *was* his life.

David prayed at all times. From the morning prayers of Psalm three to the evening prayers of Psalm four, David lived in the ebb and flow of ceaseless praying. On mountains, in caves, as a shepherd and as a king, he prayed continually before God.

David prayed in his trials. Family dysfunction, ongoing battles, kingdom politics, and emotional distress plagued David's regime; however, in rawness of spirit, David can be found crying out, "Unto thee, O LORD, do I lift up my soul" (Psalm 25:1).

David prayed in his triumphs. The true mark of a praying man is his willingness to not only pray in trouble but in triumph. Poverty of soul will incline the most carnal of saints to cry out to God, but those who genuinely love the Lord will bow after the battle is won and glorify God for His deliverance and strength.

David prayed in his transgressions. David was no perfect man. He knew the power of sin and felt full force the chastening hand of God. However, he always turned to the Lord in prayer. A praying man embraces repentance as an ongoing practice of life.

David prayed with all thanksgiving. Israel learned much of its worship through the prayer life of King David. His psalms of prayer produced mighty acts of praise among the people. Such power comes not from a man who prays, but from a praying man.

PRAYER PRINCIPLE

The difference between a man who prays and a praying man is the spirit of prayer that resides in his heart during every activity and event of life. A praying man does not just pray, but rather develops a life of prayer.

PRAYER POINTS:

- There are many people who pray that never cultivate a life of devotion to God.
- A praying man lives *in*, *through*, and *by* prayer.
- A man who prays will see prayer as an opportunity for blessing from the Lord, but a praying man sees prayer as an offering of himself unto the Lord.
- Continual prayer produces a life of fellowship with God.

PRAYER PASSAGES

- "Then went king David in, and sat before the LORD, and he said, Who am I, O Lord God? and what is my house, that thou hast brought me hitherto?" (2 Samuel 7:18).
- "As the hart panteth after the water brooks, so panteth my soul after thee, O God" (Psalm 42:1).

PRAYER PETITION

Holy and Mighty King, To be in Your presence at all times is the desire of my heart. Help me to live unto You through the spirit of prayer. May my soul long for You with passion and desire. Keep my soul near to Your side and let my life be an offering unto You in prayer.

PRAYER PONDERINGS:

Discuss the difference between a man who prays and a praying man.

_____

_____

_____

_____

_____

How does prayer cultivate a life of devotion unto God?

_____

_____

_____

_____

_____

How does one practically live in the spirit of prayer?

_____

_____

_____

_____

_____

Cite other psalms that describe the prayer life of David:

_____

_____

_____

_____

_____

PRAYER PAGE:

What I have learned today about prayer:

_____

_____

_____

_____

_____

Today I am thankful for:

_____

_____

_____

_____

_____

Today I am asking for:

_____

_____

_____

_____

_____

My confession before God today is:

_____

_____

_____

_____

_____

"I cannot pray as I would; yet I will obey,
for though my prayer be not acceptable, yet Your own
commitment is acceptable to You."

– Martin Luther

18

THE PRAYER OF

SOLOMON

HOW THE GLORY OF GOD IS
SHOWN THROUGH THE POWER OF PRAYER

Date: _____

God's glory is so magnanimous, so immeasurable that it will take all of eternity for the redeemed of the Lord to enjoy and understand it. The natural man cannot fully comprehend the awesome aura of the Almighty. Through the ages, God has presented parts and parcels of His presence to humanity, but not the entirety, not the fullness thereof. Such holy revelation would wholly consume civilization with divine flame leaving nothing of mankind but the ashes of his sinful flesh.

God does, however, on rare occasion, give glimpses of glory divine, but never apart from prayer. Thomas Brooks said, "God is an immense and infinite being, whose center is everywhere, whose circumference is nowhere." You cannot confine God's presence to a building, a closet, or a temple. He is greater than any theological description, He is grander than any religious declaration. Immense and infinite indeed, and when He decides to manifest Himself, it will be an obvious and glorious entrance, always in response to praying saints. When Jacob prayed, God came as a wrestler in the night. Who else walked in the fire with God but those praying Hebrew boys? After much beseeching, Jehovah passed by Moses in the cleft of the rock. The disciples prayed, and cloven tongues of fire swept through their souls with the enabling power of God.

Prayer precedes power. Groaning begets glory. It is only when a saint comes before God with a spirit of supplication that he can be a candidate for such divine visitation. King Solomon knew this principle well. Wisdom could have designed a temple. Wealth could have funded the project. Manpower could have laid the stones together, but only prayer, and its inherent power, could seek the face of God and dare entertain the thought that God just might show up. And show up He did…in grand fashion!

> "Now when Solomon made an end of praying, the fire came down from heaven, and consumed the burnt offering and the sacrifices; and the glory of the LORD filled the house" (2 Chronicles 7:1).

The nature of God's glory is a secret in the heart of man, but it is no secret as to what brings it down. The earthly invitation of prayer produces a heavenly manifestation of power. When God decides to show up, there will be somewhere, somehow, in some way, some saint of God supplicating for it. Humble and happy are those who catch a glimpse of it in prayer. What does His glory produce? More praying! For when Solomon and all of Israel saw His glory, they bowed themselves in prayer! Prayer brings glory, and glory brings prayer. Such is the life of a praying saint.

PRAYER PRINCIPLE

Prayer affords the child of God the opportunity to experience God's presence. His glory, or the essence of His being, produces a life of reverence, commitment, and adoration. It is prayer that gives way to such holy experience.

PRAYER POINTS:

- God cannot be confined to a place, but when He reveals Himself, He will ordain that place with His presence.
- The prerequisite for experiencing God is prayer.
- Though fleshly man cannot fully obtain or understand God's glory, he has been allotted certain glimpses.
- Our body is the temple of the Lord. The fact that He dwells within us is the hope of glory.

PRAYER PASSAGES

- "And he said, Draw not nigh hither: put off thy shoes from off thy feet, for the place whereon thou standest is holy ground" (Exodus 3:5)
- "These words spake Jesus, and lifted up his eyes to heaven, and said, Father, the hour is come; glorify thy Son, that thy Son also may glorify thee" (John 17:1).

PRAYER PETITION

Most Glorious God, To You and You alone do I offer the voice of thanksgiving and praise. Help me to sense Your Spirit and know Your presence as I pray. Meet me in that holy place and abide in me forever.

PRAYER PONDERINGS:

What words would you use to describe the glory of God?

_____

_____

_____

_____

_____

Do you believe it is possible to experience God's glory in prayer?

_____

_____

_____

_____

_____

Explain the following statement: Groaning begets glory.

_____

_____

_____

_____

_____

What else did Solomon do in preparation of building the temple?

_____

_____

_____

_____

_____

PRAYER PAGE:

What I have learned today about prayer:

_____

_____

_____

_____

_____

Today I am thankful for:

_____

_____

_____

_____

_____

Today I am asking for:

_____

_____

_____

_____

_____

My confession before God today is:

_____

_____

_____

_____

_____

"Prayer is God's ordained way to bring His miracle power to bear in human need."

− Wesley Duewel

19

THE PRAYER OF

ELIJAH

HOW EFFECTUAL, FERVENT,
RIGHTEOUS PRAYING AVAILETH MUCH

Date: _____

Seemingly out of nowhere, the prophet Elijah pops off the pages of God's Word to procure a pattern for praying. Not just any kind of praying, but effectual, fervent, righteous praying. One may think he was other-worldly had not James told us he was "a man subject to like passions as we are" (James 5:17). Like us, he was a man; unlike so many of us, he was a man of prayer.

So virtuous were his prayers that when he prayed, fire fell from heaven. So noble were his prayers that when he prayed, life was given to the dead. So passionate were his prayers that when he prayed, food was miraculously replenished. So enigmatic were his prayers that when he prayed the rain stayed from the nation for three and half years, and when he prayed again, the heaven's flooded the earth. Was Elijah like us? Yes…and no.

He was like us in that he was of born from below with the same flesh, blood, and spirit that comprises the makeup of mankind; but he was unlike so many of us in that when he prayed, he prayed with dynamite, explosive power, born from above. His prayers were not laced with poetic beauty or fanciful words, nor were they offered in long measure of speech. No religious awards were given in the publication of his prayers, but they were honored in heaven, set forth with the flame of righteousness, consumed with the very fire of God. In the classic book, *The Secret Key to Heaven*, Thomas Brooks wrote:

> "God looks not at the elegancy of your prayers, to see how neat they are; nor yet at the geometry of your prayers, to see how long they are; nor yet at the arithmetic of your prayers, to see how many they are; nor at the music of your prayers, nor yet at the sweetness of your voice, nor yet at the logic of your prayers; but at the sincerity of your prayers, to see how hearty they are."

Righteous living produces effectual praying. To be certain, there is much talking and pleading and begging going on in religious circles these days, but not much praying. The prophets of Baal were not cold nor apathetic in their altar plea. They lacked not fire nor fervency, nor fear of man; but they did lack faith and faithfulness to the true and living God.

It is, therefore, not the man who makes a scene in prayer who gets a response from God; but rather, the man who lives in holy consciousness of God outside of his prayer closet that has availing answers from above. It is the repaired altar that honors God, it is the repaired altar that God honors; even such, it is the heart of righteousness that possesses the warmth of heaven's flame.

PRAYER PRINCIPLE

It is the condition of the heart, not necessarily the content of the prayer that produces power. God is pleased to provide answers to prayer when they are offered from a holy, consecrated life.

PRAYER POINTS:

- God has designed prayer to generate spiritual power.
- Fervency and pathos alone do not guarantee answers from God in prayer.
- Power in prayer is not measured by the length, beauty, or articulation of the prayer, but rather by the spiritual condition of the one who is praying.
- When fervency coincides with righteous living, God promises availing answers to prayer.

PRAYER PASSAGES

- "Hear me when I call, O God of my righteousness: thou hast enlarged me when I was in distress; have mercy upon me, and hear my prayer" (Psalm 4:1)
- "In thee, O LORD, do I put my trust; let me never be ashamed: deliver me in thy righteousness" (Psalm 34:1).

PRAYER PETITION

Righteous and Holy God, I pray not only for fervency of heart, but for righteousness of soul. Cleanse me and keep me pure in Thy sight. Help me to walk in the precepts of Your Word and bring availing answers to my life. In Jesus name I pray, Amen.

PRAYER PONDERINGS:

What aspects of Elijah's prayer life coincides with your own?

_____

_____

_____

_____

_____

Have you experienced answers to prayer that "availeth much?"

_____

_____

_____

_____

_____

How does the condition of the heart determine answers to prayer?

_____

_____

_____

_____

_____

Can someone pray fervently but not righteously? And vice versa?

_____

_____

_____

_____

_____

PRAYER PAGE:

What I have learned today about prayer:

_____

_____

_____

_____

_____

Today I am thankful for:

_____

_____

_____

_____

Today I am asking for:

_____

_____

_____

_____

My confession before God today is:

_____

_____

_____

_____

"You should accordingly exercise your mind to remember your friends, relatives, and fellow-workers to determine if they are in need. As you remember each one so shall you in turn intercede for them. If in interceding on their behalf your spirit remains cold and dry, then you know you are not to pray for them."

– Watchman Nee

20

THE PRAYER OF

ELISHA

HOW PRAYING FOR OTHERS CAN
OPEN THEIR EYES TO THE POWER OF GOD

Date: _____

H e was the protégé of power, a prophet of miracles, a voice of truth to kings and peasants alike. Elisha was Israel's enigmatic man of God, and he had the mantle to prove it. He had prayed for a double portion of Elijah's spirit; and a careful examination of his life and ministry reveals that God answered his request in divine fashion. Elisha did everything Elijah did and then some. He raised the dead, made ax heads to float, cured leprosy, purified water springs with salt, and on more than one occasion helped rescue the nation from political defeat. Elisha not only lived in the power of the Spirit; he opened the spiritual eyes of those around him; a man of prayer always does.

Such was the case when the Syrians threatened to invade Israel. The king of Syria sent a massive army of horses and chariots to Dothan. When Elisha's servant saw the impressive legion, he was overcome with fear. However, Elisha quickly consoled him:

"And he answered, Fear not: for they that with us are more than they be with them. And Elisha prayed, and said, LORD, I pray thee, open his eyes, that he may see. And the LORD opened the eyes of the young man; and he saw; and behold, the mountain was full of horses and charities of fire round about Elisha" (2 Kings 6:16-17).

What an eye-opening prayer! As the armies of Syria were invading Israel, Elisha the prophet was invading heaven! I suppose no greater request can be made for others than to have their spiritual eyes opened to the realities and possibilities of the glory world. This is what Paul prayed for the Ephesians:

"That the God of our Lord Jesus Christ, the Father of glory, may give you wisdom and revelation in the knowledge of him: The eyes of your understanding being enlightened" (Ephesians 1:17-18).

And again, for the Colossians he prayed:

"...that ye may be filled with the knowledge of his will in all wisdom and spiritual understanding" (Colossians 1:9)

Even as natural blindness has no cure outside of God's strength, so it is with spiritual sight. Prayer is the prescription for holy enlightenment. Once the prayer order has been placed, God in His infinite power is able to wipe the natural clay from the eyes of those who cannot see. No greater gift is offered to others than the gift of sight, for in it, the unknown is unveiled, the unobtainable is in reach, and that which is not seen comes into clear focus. True prayer illuminates the blinded soul to the glory of God.

PRAYER PRINCIPLE

Prayer and supplication give way for others to have their spiritual eyes opened to the realities of God. No greater act of kindness is bestowed upon a soul than when another soul beseeches heaven for the impartation of wisdom and knowledge.

PRAYER POINTS:

- There is spiritual activity going on in the world.
- The natural sight of man cannot see nor understand the spiritual realities of God.
- Praying for others to know or "see" the power of God is essential for their spiritual well-being.
- The goal for spiritual enlightenment is for God to be obeyed, trusted, and glorified.

PRAYER PASSAGES

- "Call unto me, and I will answer thee, and show thee great and mighty things, which thou knowest not" (Jeremiah 33:3).
- "Beloved, I wish above all things that thou mayest prosper and be in health, even as thy soul prospereth" (3 John 1:2).

PRAYER PETITION

Great and Mighty God, What a privilege it is to pray for others. I ask that You enlighten the spiritual eyes of my friends and family. Give them knowledge of Your will and Your Word. Cause them to see Your goodness and grace. Comfort them with Your divine presence.

PRAYER PONDERINGS:

When you pray for others what is the primary objective?

_____

_____

_____

_____

_____

How does the enemy distract God's people from knowing His will?

_____

_____

_____

_____

_____

Read Ephesians 3:14-21 and pray this prayer for someone you love.

_____

_____

_____

_____

_____

What happens to someone when their spiritual eyes are opened?

_____

_____

_____

_____

_____

PRAYER PAGE:

What I have learned today about prayer:

_____
_____
_____
_____
_____

Today I am thankful for:

_____
_____
_____
_____
_____

Today I am asking for:

_____
_____
_____
_____
_____

My confession before God today is:

_____
_____
_____
_____
_____

"I never prayed sincerely and honestly for anything but it came; at some time, the matter how distant the day, somehow, in some shape, probably the last I should have devised, it came."

– Adoniram Judson

21

THE PRAYER OF

HEZEKIAH

HOW GOD BRINGS ANSWERS TO PRAYER
IN ACCORDANCE WITH OUR ASKING

Date: _____

If prayer is not asking and receiving then it is nothing at all. As a gracious and loving Father, God invites us to make our requests known unto Him, to pour out our souls before His throne. He has designed prayer within the framework of asking, seeking, and knocking. It is His good pleasure to give good gifts to His children, to bestow upon them the desires of their hearts. If we have not, it is because we have failed to ask. Asking is the order of His kingdom, it is how the distribution of answers are allocated to His people. This is the fundamental premise of prayer.

King Hezekiah not only understood this truth, he lived by it, literally. He was a faithful king who ruled in Judah serving the Lord with integrity of heart. Though he was a righteous man, he became extremely sick, sick unto death. Isaiah the prophet visited Hezekiah on his sick bed and told him to "set thine house in order; for thou shalt die, and not live" (2 Kings 20:1). In response to the dreaded word of the prophet, Hezekiah turned his face to the wall and prayed with tears:

> "I beseech thee, O LORD, remember now how I have walked before thee in truth and with a perfect heart, and have done that which is good in thy sight. And Hezekiah wept sore" (2 Kings 20:3).

Before Isaiah could even leave the middle court of the palace, the Lord told the prophet to return to the king with these words:

> "I have heard thy prayer, I have seen thy tears: behold, I will heal thee: on the third day thou shalt go up unto the house of the LORD. And I will add unto thy days fifteen years..." (2 Kings 20:5-6)

Great is the mystery of God's providence in terms of answering our prayers. Be certain, God orders the events of our lives, in Him we live, move, and have our being. However, within the context of His sovereignty, He allows us to ask, nay, He bids us to ask; and in the asking He answers according to the request. Had not Hezekiah prayed, then the prophecy would have come to pass, and he would have died. But instead of dying, Hezekiah turned to God in prayer. In response, God added fifteen years to his life thus fulfilling the promise, "Ask and ye shall receive."

Adoniram Judson said, "I never prayed sincerely and honestly for anything but it came; at some time, no matter how distant the day, somehow, in some shape, probably the last I should have devised, it came." The only thing preventing us from living more enriched lives could very well be our failure to ask for it.

PRAYER PRINCIPLE

Though sovereign in every sense of the word, God bids us to make our petition known before Him; in His goodness, He answers according to our asking. The whole constitution of prayer consists of one party asking and the other party giving.

PRAYER POINTS:

- Distress, disease, and even death drives us to prayer and awakens our faith toward God.
- Prayer consists of many things, but the divine structure of prayer involves asking and receiving.
- God, in providence, can change situations that would have remained unchanged without His intervening.
- Prayer moves the hand that moves the world.

PRAYER PASSAGES

- "I called upon the LORD in distress: the LORD answered me, and set me in a large place" (Psalm 118:5).
- "O Lord, by these things men live, and in all these things is the life of my spirit: so shalt thou recover me, and make me to live" (Isaiah 38:16).

PRAYER PETITION

Dear Lord, You are the Healer of my heart and soul. In You I live, move, and have my being. I ask You to give me the wisdom to know what to ask for. Give me the knowledge of Your will and give me faith to believe. Let my requests come before You, answer me, O Lord, when I call.

PRAYER PONDERINGS:

Do you find it difficult to ask God for certain things? If so, why?

_____

_____

_____

_____

_____

Describe the relationship between God's sovereignty and our asking.

_____

_____

_____

_____

_____

What situations in your life has God changed through prayer?

_____

_____

_____

_____

_____

Do you believe "Prayer moves the hand that moves the world"?

_____

_____

_____

_____

_____

PRAYER PAGE:

What I have learned today about prayer:

_____

_____

_____

_____

_____

Today I am thankful for:

_____

_____

_____

_____

_____

Today I am asking for:

_____

_____

_____

_____

_____

My confession before God today is:

_____

_____

_____

_____

_____

"The most difficult part of intercession is taking the time and effort to discover what to pray. Asking is the easy part."

– Lee Brase

22

THE PRAYER OF

JABEZ

HOW PRAYER IMPARTS DIVINE FAVOR
IN THE LIVES OF ORDINARY PEOPLE

Date: _____

The course and events of history have been shaped by the prayers of God's people. Notable in Scripture are those men and women who supplicated in miraculous fashion, receiving by the hand of God great answers to their prayers. Elijah prayed fire down from heaven. Hannah prayed a child into her womb. Solomon prayed until the glory of God filled the temple. Such names are known to us in Scripture because their dynamic prayers were known to God in heaven. But what about those lesser-known individuals who sought the favor of God? Did God work in their lives in any lesser fashion? Does God hear and answer the prayers of no-named, ordinary folks like you and me?

Jabez would affirm that He does. Jabez was not a king who sat on a throne, he was not a prophet who worked miracles, he was not a patriarch on the list of great faith. He was an ordinary man who simply prayed to an extraordinary God for divine favor.

No detail is given of his occupation, personality, or cultural influence. He was just a man listed in Judah's genealogy among many other names. However, unlike many others, he was "more honorable than his brethren" for when he prayed, he asked for God's blessings upon his life.

"And Jabez called on the God of Israel, saying, Oh that thou wouldest bless me indeed, and enlarge my coast, and that thine hand might be with me, and that thou wouldest keep me from evil, that it may not grieve me! And God granted him that which he requested" (1 Chronicles 4:10).

Short, simple, and succinct, this prayer intentionally sought the favor of God. Jabez asked for God's provision and got it, for God's presence and got it, for God's protection and got it. The Lord granted him everything he requested.

The prayer of Jabez reminds us that God imparts favor in the lives of ordinary people. Samuel Chadwick said:

Ordinary people may pray about commonplace things, and the answer to their prayers may be in an enlightened mind, a triumphant soul, a steadfast faith, and a holy life. There may be no miraculous incidents, but prayer lifts the lowliest and most ordinary life to the exalted plane of the supernatural, and this is the greatest miracle of all."

Prayer is not an exercise only suitable for prophet-talkers and water-walkers. God has designed prayer so that even the most informal, unlearned child has access. At the throne of grace, His favor awaits…for kings and peasants, for preachers and paupers, for the famed and the unknown.

PRAYER PRINCIPLE

God desires to impart His blessings upon the most ordinary of individuals. Such blessings are contingent upon our willingness to live honorable lives and to pursue Him in prayer and supplication.

PRAYER POINTS:

- The events of history are largely formed and established through the prayers of God's people.
- Ordinary people have just as much access to God in prayer as those individuals who have done great things in history.
- God permits us to ask for His favor when we pray.
- The blessings and favor of God are given in response to those who live honorable and righteous lives.

PRAYER PASSAGES

- "I am the LORD thy God, which brought thee out of the land of Egypt: open thy mouth wide, and I will fill it" (Psalm 81:10).
- "And this is the confidence that we have in him, that, if we ask anything according to his will, he heareth us" (1 John 5:14).

PRAYER PETITION

Gracious Lord, Even as Jabez sought the blessings and favor of God for his life, I pray that You will continue to impart Your daily benefits in mine. Help me to live in an honorable fashion. Give me the desire to pursue righteousness and holiness; and that You would bless me indeed.

PRAYER PONDERINGS:

In your own words, write out a prayer like the prayer of Jabez.

_____

_____

_____

_____

_____

Do you think there is biblical ground to ask for God's prosperity?

_____

_____

_____

_____

_____

What does it mean to have the favor of God?

_____

_____

_____

_____

_____

Are there contingencies in receiving and living in God's blessings?

_____

_____

_____

_____

_____

PRAYER PAGE:

What I have learned today about prayer:

_____

_____

_____

_____

_____

Today I am thankful for:

_____

_____

_____

_____

_____

Today I am asking for:

_____

_____

_____

_____

_____

My confession before God today is:

_____

_____

_____

_____

_____

"There is a difference between God searching me and me searching myself. I may search my heart and pronounce it all right, but when God searches me as with a lighted candle, a good many things will come to light that perhaps I knew nothing about."

– D.L. Moody

23

THE PRAYER OF

MANASSEH

HOW GOD EXTENDS MERCY TO
THOSE WHO HUMBLY CRY OUT IN PRAYER

Date: _____

Only twelve years old when he became king, Manasseh ruled in Judah for fifty five years. Instead of following in the righteous footsteps of his father Hezekiah, Manasseh wholly pursued idolatry, corruption, and spiritual darkness. He "did that which was evil in the sight of the LORD, like unto the abominations of the heathen" (2 Chronicles 33:2). In every sense of the word, Manasseh was wicked. Scripture tells us:

- He rebuilt monuments of idols torn down by his father.

- He constructed altars to Baalim.

- He made idols in the holy place of God.

- He caused Israel to engage in child sacrifice.

- He was involved with witchcraft and sorcery.

God gave Manasseh an opportunity to repent, but the king refused to hear the call of God. Therefore, the Lord sent the Assyrian army and bound him with thorns and fetters and carried him to Babylon.

In despair of soul, Manasseh turned to the true and living God for deliverance and began to pray:

> "And when he was in affliction, he besought the LORD his God, and humbled himself greatly before the God of his fathers, And prayed unto him, and he was entreated of him, and heard his supplication, and brought him again to Jerusalem into his kingdom. Then Manasseh knew that the LORD he was God" (2 Chronicles 33:12-14).

Prayer is a precious ointment to the sin-sick soul. It calls out for relief in the heavenlies, it waits anxiously for the balm of grace to be applied. Its tears of repentance go forth as ambassadors seeking refuge from the King of Glory. It cries, it begs, it pleads for mercy, knowing that mercy is its only cure.

Such desperation always gains the ear of God. It is not the whole that needs a physician, it is the sick. And when the sick sinner begins to moan in the spirit, the mercy of the Lord is poured into the wounded heart. Heaven's Healer is always drawn toward contrition. He specializes in restoring broken bones and broken hearts and even broken kings.

True praying brings real mercy which results in genuine conversion which produces holy living. In response to his answered prayer, Manasseh took away his strange gods, removed the idols from the temple, repaired the altar of the LORD, and sacrificed offerings thereon. Manasseh's prayer of repentance became legendary throughout all of Israel as a testimony of God's mercy and grace. Prayer was and always will be God's means to impart forgiveness.

PRAYER PRINCIPLE

When God draws a sinner to prayer, He stands ready to impart mercy and grace to their repentant hearts. When an individual sees their sinful condition before the Lord, then, and only then, will they be ready to cry out for forgiveness.

PRAYER POINTS:

- The power of sin can take an individual down a dangerous and dark path.
- The price of sin is greater than our ability to pay.
- It is only in contrition and heartbreak can a sinner or saint receive mercy from God.
- God uses prayer as the means to bring healing, forgiveness and restoration in the lives of His people.

PRAYER PASSAGES

- "Turn thee unto me, and have mercy upon me; for I am desolate and afflicted" (Psalm 25:16).
- "And I will shew mercies unto you, that he may have mercy upon you, and cause you to return to your own land" (Jeremiah 42:12).

PRAYER PETITION

Holy God, I come to You with bitter tears of sorrow. I have no hope but You, no consolation but in Thee. Hear my cry, cleanse my heart, purify my love for You. Keep me from the temptations of sins and guard my mind with righteous and holy living. Extend Your mercy to me. Amen.

PRAYER PONDERINGS:

Do you believe Manasseh was saved prior to his prayer?

_____

_____

_____

_____

_____

In your own experience, how has sin affected your prayer life?

_____

_____

_____

_____

_____

In your own experience, how has your prayer life affected your sin?

_____

_____

_____

_____

_____

Can God restore anyone from sin, no matter how severe? Explain.

_____

_____

_____

_____

_____

PRAYER PAGE:

What I have learned today about prayer:

_____

_____

_____

_____

_____

Today I am thankful for:

_____

_____

_____

_____

Today I am asking for:

_____

_____

_____

_____

My confession before God today is:

_____

_____

_____

_____

"The supreme thing is worship. The attitude of worship is the attitude of a subject bent before the King... the fundamental thought is that of prostration, of bowing down."

– G. Campbell Morgan

24

THE PRAYER OF

JEHOSHAPHAT

HOW PRAYER AND PRAISE ARE
THE GREATEST WEAPONS OF WARFARE

Date: _____

So closely related are prayer and praise that you can scarcely have one without the other. The apostle Paul said, "Be careful for nothing; but in everything by prayer and supplication with thanksgiving let your requests be made known unto God" (Philippians 4:6). The highest expression of worship is formed when the saint of God releases his utterances before the throne with a thankful heart. The holy constitution of prayer is built upon these two commands, "Rejoice evermore. Pray without ceasing" (1 Thessalonians 5:16-17). Prayer and praise are inseparable because they depend upon one another for strength. Prayer is an act of worship; and worship, in its purest form, finds its bedrock in prayer. They exist as a double-edged sword in the fight of faith.

There is no better example of prayer and praise than in the life of King Jehoshaphat. As the Moabites and Ammonites joined their alliances against Israel, Jehoshaphat knew he was outnumbered and outmanned. Instead of beefing up his military or devising a strategic plan of attack, the king of Israel went to the temple and prayed. Not only did he pray, he proclaimed a fast and caused all the cities of Judah to seek the Lord in prayer.

God provided an answer. Instead of warring against the enemy, the were simply instructed to worship the Lord God. They would not win the battle with soldiers but rather with singers. As the enemy prepared their weapons of warfare, Jehoshaphat made ready his choir:

> "And when they began to sing and to praise, the Lord set ambushments against the children of Ammon, Moab, and mount Seir, which were come against Judah; and they were smitten" (2 Chronicles 20:22).

As God's people praised the Lord, the Lord fought on their behalf and destroyed the enemy. Instead of raising their swords, they simply raised their voices; and as the people brought their voices before the Lord, the Lord brought victory before the people. Such is the blessing and benefit of prayer and praise.

Wherever you find a praying saint, you will find a thankful heart. Supplication begets singing and singing brings supplication. "Continue in prayer," said the apostle, "and watch in the same with thanksgiving" (Colossians 4:20). Nothing is more threatening to the enemy than when God's soldiers arm themselves with the weaponry of prayer and praise. Such an approach to warfare always draws the Lord to the fight. When the Lord shows up for battle, there is nothing for the saint of God to do but to watch, worship, and win.

PRAYER PRINCIPLE

The twin powers of prayer and praise arm the child of God in the battles of life. The enemy is hard-pressed to stand against a saint who prays without ceasing and who rejoices ever more.

PRAYER POINTS:

- Human intellect and ingenuity are no forces against the awesome power of the enemy.
- Prayer should be an immediate response in every conflict.
- A godly man will not only turn to the Lord in prayer, he will cause others to join him in the fight.
- The attitude of prayer should be one of thanksgiving and gratitude. One cannot pray without offering praise.

PRAYER PASSAGES

- "Then said David to the Philistine, Thou comest to me with a sword, and with a spear, and with a shield: but I come to thee in the name of the LORD of hosts, the God of the armies of Israel," (1 Samuel 17:45).
- "In everything give thanks for this is the will of God in Christ Jesus concerning you" (1 Thessalonians 5:18).

PRAYER PETITION

To the Lord of Hosts, I worship You and thank You for Your mighty hand. You have prevailed in the battle. You are strong against the enemy. You have brought victory to my soul. I lift up my voice to You in praise and sing glory and honor to Your name!

PRAYER PONDERINGS:

How does gratitude affect your attitude in prayer?

_____

_____

_____

_____

_____

Does worship and praise have a rightful place in your prayers?

_____

_____

_____

_____

_____

Read Colossians 3:16 and discuss what it means to sing to the Lord.

_____

_____

_____

_____

_____

Is it really possible to give thanks in everything? How so?

_____

_____

_____

_____

_____

PRAYER PAGE:

What I have learned today about prayer:

_____

_____

_____

_____

_____

Today I am thankful for:

_____

_____

_____

_____

_____

Today I am asking for:

_____

_____

_____

_____

_____

My confession before God today is:

_____

_____

_____

_____

_____

"I poured out my soul before God, and arose from my knees in peace, because the trouble that was in the soul was in believing prayer cast upon God, and thus, I was kept in peace, though I saw it to be the will of God to remain far away from the work."

– George Mueller

25

THE PRAYER OF

ASA

HOW PRAYER BRINGS
PEACE AND REST TO THE SOUL

Date: _____

The reign of king Asa in Judah was fairly uneventful. Known as a good king, he did that which was right in the eyes of the Lord. During his tenure as king, "the land was quiet ten years" (2 Chronicles 14:1). He took away the altars of strange gods, broke down images and cut down the groves. He commanded the people to "seek the Lord God of their fathers" and to live by the commandments of the law. As a result of his righteous leadership, Israel enjoyed a decade of peace and tranquility. The Bible says:

- "the kingdom was quiet before him" (2 Chronicles 14:5)
- "the land had rest" (2 Chronicles 14:6)
- "The LORD had given him rest" (2 Chronicles 14:6)
- The Lord "gave rest on every side" (2 Chronicles 14:7)

All of that changed, however, when Zerah the Ethiopian disturbed the peace of Asa's kingdom. With thousands of foot soldiers and hundreds of chariots, he invaded Israel and sought to destroy them.

Asa turned to the Lord in prayer and simply cried out, "Help us, O LORD our God; for we have rest on thee, and in thy name we go against this multitude" (2 Chronicles 14:11). The Lord heard his simple prayer and smote the Ethiopians until they fled from king Asa. Israel's ability to rest in the land was contingent upon their willingness to rest upon the Lord. God's provision for Asa's petition is the same response He gives to all of those who desire to experience divine peace. The apostle Paul said:

> "Be careful for nothing; but in every thing by prayer and supplication with thanksgiving let your requests be made known unto God. And the peace of God, which passeth all understanding, shall keep your hearts and minds through Christ Jesus" (Philippians 4:6-7).

Here we find a strong correlation between God's peace and our prayers. Indescribable, inexplicable peace is offered to the saint of God who makes it his practice to pray "in everything" about everything, and for everything. A glorious phenomenon occurs when we make our requests known before God; He provides rest in the wrestling, solitude in the supplication, peace in the petition.

His peace, so divine and unexplainable, offers a strong defense against the anxieties of this life. When we transfer our cares upon Him, He indelibly fills our souls, undeniably guards our hearts, and indefinitely protects our minds. Prayer, then, becomes the key that unlocks the gateway of His grace, the doorway of His deliverance, and the pathway of His peace. Such peace may never change the situation of the one praying, but it always changes the one praying regardless of the situation.

PRAYER PRINCIPLE

When a believer commits himself or herself to the habit of prayer, God will keep their hearts and minds through Christ, thus causing them to experience a peace which passes understanding, even in the most tempestuous of circumstances.

PRAYER POINTS:

- Prayer does not necessarily keep the enemy away; if anything, it may cause him to fight harder against the soul.
- Prayer should not be a last resort, but an ongoing practice.
- God invites us to cast our cares upon Him in prayer.
- In exchange for our cares, the Lord promises to keep our hearts and minds with an undeniable peace.

PRAYER PASSAGES

- "Thou wilt keep him in perfect peace, whose mind is stayed on thee; because he trusteth in thee" (Isaiah 26:3).
- "I exhort therefore, that, first of all, supplications, prayers, intercessions, and giving of thanks, be made for all men; For kings, and for all that are in authority; that we may a lead quiet and peaceable life in all godliness and honesty" (1 Timothy 2:1-2).

PRAYER PETITION

Prince of Peace, I bless You for the peace that You give me during the most difficult seasons of life. Help me to cast my cares upon You, and in exchange, guard my heart and mind against fear and doubt.

PRAYER PONDERINGS:

Write out a clear definition of the peace of God:

_____

_____

_____

_____

_____

How does God grant peace to us when we pray?

_____

_____

_____

_____

_____

Can a believer experience peace who does not habitually pray?

_____

_____

_____

_____

_____

Do you think the unrest in our society is due to lack of prayer?

_____

_____

_____

_____

_____

PRAYER PAGE:

What I have learned today about prayer:

_____

_____

_____

_____

_____

Today I am thankful for:

_____

_____

_____

_____

_____

Today I am asking for:

_____

_____

_____

_____

_____

My confession before God today is:

_____

_____

_____

_____

_____

"God's way of answering the Christian's prayer for more patience, experience, hope, and love often is to put him into the furnace of affliction."

– Richard Cecil

26

THE PRAYER OF

JOB

HOW PRAYER RECONCILES SUFFERING
AND THE SOVEREIGNTY OF GOD

Date: _____

If the intensity of one's prayer is measured by the severity of one's travail, then Job must have been the most passionate petitioner in the Old Testament. Outside of his integrity, Job lost all that he had. He described his ailments as the "slaying of God." Who can really fathom such agony of soul? How does a man walk away from the burial plots of ten children? How do you recover from the immediate and total loss of livestock and livelihood? What does it feel like to bear in the body the boils of Satan?

Job's story is one of sovereignty, suffering, and supplication. It can be condensed into three statements: God permits; Satan plagues; and man pleads. The divine inner workings of such profound mysteries will never be fully reconciled in the finite comprehension of humanity, but one thing is certain about Job's suffering: In it, God was sought, the devil was fought, and man was wrought for the glory of the most High. How harmonious and beautiful it is when prayer and suffering dance together to the melody of God's sovereign song. How fragrant is the rose that pierces with its thorn! How lovely is the lily in the lowlands of life! Only providence can prevail in such ponderings. It is not for man to determine the outcome or forecasts of his life; it is simply his responsibility to seek the Lord and surrender, as his sole desire, to the purposes of God.

So, Job danced with God in prayer. He made his closet among the briar patch. He sat down in the depths of the valley and began crying, searching, hoping to discover the divine purpose in his pain. Instead, he found himself surrounded by a grievous companion and miserable comforters. He probed into the mysteries of God's nature, God's creation, and God's rationale in suffering. None of those enquiries provided relief. It was only when Job prayed for his friends that he received by the hand of the Lord a double portion of what he lost.

The prayer of Job, perhaps more than anything else, teaches us a great deal about trust. Either man is God and can rely upon his own strength and wisdom to persevere through the sufferings of this world, or God is God and He works all things for His glory and exaltation. God's prerogatives in the affairs of mankind are just that...God's; they belong to Him to execute as He deems necessary. One may look at the life of Job and think how wretched and miserable it must have been to dance with God in such sorrow of song; but the truth is, the greater tragedy would have been to never danced with God at all. And for this reason, God gives us prayer, His greatest gift in the groanings of life.

PRAYER PRINCIPLE

God in His sovereignty allows suffering and sorrow to exist in this fallen world as a means for mankind to call out to God for relief. As we yield to God through prayer, we learn to accept His will, even when we do not fully understand it.

PRAYER POINTS:

- Suffering is part of life and cannot be avoided.
- God allows suffering to exist to display His authority and dominion over Satan.
- Sovereignty and suffering worked together in a man's life to develop trust and dependence upon the Lord.
- God doesn't require that we understand all His purposes, but He does desire for us to yield to them.

PRAYER PASSAGES

- "Though he slay me, yet will I trust in him: but I will maintain mine own ways before him" (Job 13:15)
- "And the LORD turned the captivity of Job, when he prayed for his friends: also the LORD gave Job twice as much as he had before." (Job 42:10).

PRAYER PETITION

Heavenly Father, It is difficult at times to ascertain all that You are doing in the world and in my life. However, I do trust You and confidently know that You intend to work all things for Your glory. Conform my will to Yours and help me to yield to Your holy purposes.

PRAYER PONDERINGS:

Why do you think there is so much suffering in the world?

_____

_____

_____

_____

_____

How can you reconcile the sovereignty of God in the hurt and pain?

_____

_____

_____

_____

_____

Why do you think God restored Job when he prayed for his friends?

_____

_____

_____

_____

_____

How did God triumph over Satan in Job's affliction?

_____

_____

_____

_____

_____

PRAYER PAGE:

What I have learned today about prayer:

_____
_____
_____
_____
_____

Today I am thankful for:

_____
_____
_____
_____
_____

Today I am asking for:

_____
_____
_____
_____
_____

My confession before God today is:

_____
_____
_____
_____
_____

*"It is the highest activity of the human soul,
and therefore, it is at the same time the ultimate test
of a man's spiritual condition. There is nothing that
tells the truth about us as Christian people
so much as our prayer life."*

– Martyn Lloyd Jones

27

THE PRAYER OF

ISAIAH

HOW HONESTY IS AN ESSENTIAL
ELEMENT IN THE LIFE OF PRAYER

Date: _____

Nothing is more revolting before the Lord than a man who prays with a pretentious spirit. The flowery and fashioned prayer of the Pharisee echoes through the temple corridors with spiritual conceit, religious snobbery, and foolish pride. It may be convincing and impressive to the onlookers, but it never fools God. He sees past the piety, the fasting, and the almsgiving. He knows that within the beauty of the white sepulcher, lies the bones of a dead man. What a fitting description of the hypocrite's prayer, full of exterior beauty, but lifeless and unresponsive in the holy place of God.

It is the humble and honest prayer that wins the applause of heaven. It is the cry of the sinner for mercy, the pleading of the transgressor for grace that gains the Priestly ear. The Lord said of praying, "for every one that exalteth himself shall be abased; and he that humbleth himself shall be exalted" (Luke 18:14).

Isaiah the prophet had been both, exalted and abased, high and lowly, pretentious and sincere. However, when he entered the exalted presence of the true King of Israel, he discovered there was no hiding behind his religious pedigrees. His sermons, his prophecies, his oratory skills could not relieve him from the fiery guilt he felt in his heart. His own lips betrayed him:

> "Woe is me! for I am undone; because I am a man of unclean lips, and I dwell in the midst of a people of unclean lips: for mine eyes have seen the King, the LORD of hosts" (Isaiah 6:5).

Here we find Isaiah, just as the lowly publican, with lifted eyes to heaven, beating his chest, crying out for mercy from the true and living God. His lips are unclean because his heart is undone. Instead of skirting the issue with religious rhetoric, Isaiah pleads for the coal of the altar to burn out the sinfulness in his life.

This is raw. This is real. This is prayer.

In his book, *Prevailing Prayer*, D.L. Moody said:

> There is a difference between God searching me and me searching myself. I may search my heart and pronounce it all right, but when God searches me as with a lighted candle, a good many things will come to light that perhaps I knew nothing about."

To truly pray means to pray truly, as true as you truly are; the real you praying to the real God. It means to eliminate the facades, escape the excuses, and expose the heart as it is before the Lord. When a man honestly prays, God, in return, honestly hears.

PRAYER PRINCIPLE

When a believer comes before the Lord with an honest and open heart, the Lord will honor that prayer by extending to the saint a measure of mercy and grace.

PRAYER POINTS:

- The transparent heart always has company with God.
- God addresses our heart in the areas of sinful contention.
- When a believer willingly acknowledges and confesses his sin, the Lord is quick to supply a remedy of forgiveness.
- Honesty in prayer will position the believer to be used in the service of the Lord.

PRAYER PASSAGES

- "Also I heard the voice of the Lord saying, Whom shall I send, and who will go for us? Then said I, Here am I; send me" (Isaiah 6:8)
- "Pray for us: for we trust we have a good conscience, in all things willingly to live honestly." (Hebrews 13:8).

PRAYER PETITION

Kind and Gracious Savior, help me to come before You with sincerity of heart. I hold nothing back; I bring all my faults and failures. I plead for mercy and grace. May you purge my unclean lips with the coals from Your altar and may the sacrifice of Christ's atoning blood speak on my behalf. In His name, and for His sake, I pray, Amen.

PRAYER PONDERINGS:

How does sin hinder our prayers?

_____

_____

_____

_____

_____

Why is it easier to point out the transgressions of others?

_____

_____

_____

_____

_____

Do you think you are honest with God when you pray?

_____

_____

_____

_____

_____

God enlisted Isaiah after he confessed his sins. Why was it this way?

_____

_____

_____

_____

_____

PRAYER PAGE:

What I have learned today about prayer:

_____

_____

_____

_____

_____

Today I am thankful for:

_____

_____

_____

_____

_____

Today I am asking for:

_____

_____

_____

_____

_____

My confession before God today is:

_____

_____

_____

_____

_____

*"All vital praying makes a drain
on a man's vitality. True intercession is
a sacrifice, a bleeding sacrifice."*
— J.H. Jowett

28

THE PRAYER OF

JEREMIAH

HOW PRAYER AFFECTS THE
EMOTIONAL STATE OF THE BELIEVER

Date: _____

Rare is the mother who delivers a child without emotion. The agony of life wrestles within her womb touching every nerve of her being. Her sensitivity is heightened, her feelings are raw, and her anticipation is so great that nothing will relieve her strain but the embrace of a grappling newborn. Emotion begets emotion, for when the child is delivered, it too, is overcome with the miracle of the moment. Grasping for breath, shocked by the light, surprised by touch, the babe cries with every instinctual feeling given to him by God. It yearns for contact. It longs for embrace. In joyful agony and in agonizing joy, mother holds babe and babe clings to mother. Life is delivered, life is born, life is felt.

In all its complexities and nuances, prayer, too is conceived and born with spiritual emotion. To pray, and not feel it, is foreign to the delivery process. When prayer is imparted in the soul's womb and then delivered before the holy seat of God, there must, of necessity be a striking of the nerve, a moving of the heart, a stirring of the spirit. Be certain, a man who prays with feeling alone may never truly pray, but if a man truly prays, there will be some feeling, some excitement in the soul.

Jeremiah delivered his prayers in such fashion. Known as the weeping prophet, he lamented his soul continuously before God. Unlike other Old Testament saints, Jeremiah's prayer life was not characterized by a solitary moment of supplication, but rather by the manner in which he prayed. Appointed as God's mouthpiece during the time of destruction, Jeremiah saw the sorrow of his people as they were taken away into captivity. Hear the agony of his prayers as he called to God:

> "Mine eye trickleth down, and ceaseth not, without intermission, Till the LORD look down, and behold from heaven. Mine eye afflicteth mine heart because of all the daughters of my city. Waters flowed over mine head; then said, I am cut off. I called upon thy name, O LORD, out of the low dungeon" (Lamentations 3:49-54).

Jeremiah's prayer exhibited the emotional state of both mother and child. In motherly fashion, he wept before God until his prayer was born; and like a babe, he cried out with such vulnerability and sorrow that only a divine Parent could calm his fears.

It is here we find the true essence of prayer. Prayer is more than words; it is the offering and outpouring of the soul. It is not only meant to be spoken; it is meant to be felt. Prayer is not just a religious exercise; it is a real experience intertwined with real emotion and real feelings offered to a real God who really hears.

PRAYER PRINCIPLE

Prayer should never be void of emotion or feeling. Praying with a burden, with the spirit of agony, creates an authenticity before God that transcends religious rhetoric or recitation.

PRAYER POINTS:

- The travail of prayer is accompanied by a variety of emotions and feelings.
- Distress of spirit can be a motivating factor in prayer.
- Praying with a burden is a healthy practice for the saint.
- True prayer is designed to be felt, not just offered.

PRAYER PASSAGES

- "Remember, O LORD, what is come upon us: for consider, and behold our reproach. Our inheritance is turned to strangers, our houses to aliens. We are orphans and fatherless, our mothers are as widows" (Lamentations 5:1-3)
- "And being in agony he prayed more earnestly: and his sweat was as it were great drops of blood failing down to the ground." (Luke 22:44).

PRAYER PETITION

Heavenly Father, I come to You with all my being. I am helpless without You. I am hopeless in this world without Your presence. May my tears be a language of understanding to You. Hear the cry of my soul and as a babe that reaches for its mother, let me long for Your embrace.

PRAYER PONDERINGS:

In your opinion, what does it mean to pray with emotion?

_____

_____

_____

_____

_____

Have you ever agonized with God? If so, over what?

_____

_____

_____

_____

_____

Does praying with emotion and agony agree with your personality?

_____

_____

_____

_____

_____

How does faith factor into the emotional aspect of prayer?

_____

_____

_____

_____

_____

PRAYER PAGE:

What I have learned today about prayer:

_____
_____
_____
_____
_____

Today I am thankful for:

_____
_____
_____
_____
_____

Today I am asking for:

_____
_____
_____
_____
_____

My confession before God today is:

_____
_____
_____
_____
_____

"There is no way that Christians, in a private capacity, can do so much to promote the work of God and advance the kingdom of Christ as by prayer."

– Jonathan Edwards

29

THE PRAYER OF

DANIEL

HOW THE HABIT OF PRAYER BUILDS
A LIFE OF COURAGE AND CONVICTION

Date: _____

Prayer, above all is else, is the most valued commodity in the believer's treasury, the most illustrious gem in the storehouse of the saints. It should be no surprise, then, that Satan as a thief, breaks into the prayer closet and tries to take away the one thing that enriches the faith of a child of God. "A Christian is well able to count the stars of heaven, and to number the sands of the sea," said Thomas Brooks, "as he is able to number up the several devices and sleights that Satan uses to obstruct the soul's private approaches to God." The enemy hates prayer because prayer hates the enemy; it outpowers his weaponry, it outsmarts his trickery, and it outdoes his robbery.

Prayer develops faith, it disciplines the will, it delights the spirit, it defends the mind, it directs the feet, it deploys the hands, it discerns the heart, it dissects the soul, and it defeats the devil. No wonder he strategically hinders God's people from prayer.

Such was the case in the life of Daniel. As a young man living among heathens in a pagan society, he was surrounded by carnal indulgences, idolatry worship, and political corruption. His colleagues in the kingdom not only despised the righteous devotion he had to the God of Israel; they equally hated the fact that he had favor with the king of Babylon. Wanting to remove Daniel from his position, they issued a decree forbidding prayer to anyone but Darius. Without hesitation or pause, Daniel went to his prayer closet, opened the windows, set his face toward Jerusalem, and poured out his heart to God in prayer...not once, not twice, but three times a day, as he had previously done. This was not only his habit; this was his life's conviction; and conviction does not rely on permission. Daniel did not need a permit from the governor of Babylon, he already had a warrant from the God of heaven. Samuel Chadwick noted:

> "The habit of prayer implies a certain attitude to life. It predicates God and recognizes his sovereignty over all. It submits all things to his will, rehearses all things in his presence, judges all things by his standards of values, and lives by faith in him. Prayer is the essence and test out the godly life. Who can measure its influence upon mind and character, or estimate it's value in practical wisdom and dexterous skill?"

The man or woman who persistently prays with heartfelt devotion to God will not be easily thwarted nor overcome when the enemy goes on the attack. They find victory in the moment of opposition because had been praying before the moment came.

PRAYER PRINCIPLE

When believers live in consistent and habitual prayer, they are not easily overthrown by the enemy's devices. They build their spiritual capital on the resources of prayer. Their courage and faith cannot be compromised by worldly influence or pressure.

PRAYER POINTS:

- Most people are not aware of the spiritual efforts made by Satan to keep them away from prayer.
- Prayer is where the battle is won in our lives.
- Cultural trends, popular opinion, and political legislation should never supersede our spiritual obligations.
- Conviction and courage are cultivated through prayer.

PRAYER PASSAGES

- "Then these men assembled, and found Daniel praying and making supplication before his God" (Daniel 6:11).
- "Deliver me from mine enemies, O my God: defend me from them that rise up against me. Deliver me from the workers of iniquity, and save me from bloody men" (Psalm 59:1-2).

PRAYER PETITION

Mighty God, You are able to overcome my enemy. You are stronger, more powerful, and capable to bring my soul out of the pit. It is my desire to build a life of courage and conviction; not to yield to the influence and pressures of this world. Resolve my heart in prayer.

PRAYER PONDERINGS:

How does a believer living in this world resemble the life of Daniel?

_____

_____

_____

_____

_____

Why does Satan work tirelessly to keep us from prayer?

_____

_____

_____

_____

_____

How does prayer develop courage and conviction?

_____

_____

_____

_____

_____

Discuss how habitual and continual prayer strengthens faith.

_____

_____

_____

_____

_____

PRAYER PAGE:

What I have learned today about prayer:

_____

_____

_____

_____

_____

Today I am thankful for:

_____

_____

_____

_____

_____

Today I am asking for:

_____

_____

_____

_____

_____

My confession before God today is:

_____

_____

_____

_____

_____

"Even pagan savages cry out to someone or something to aid them in times of danger and disaster and distress. How much more should we that know the true God."

– The Kneeling Christian

30

THE PRAYER OF

JONAH

HOW PRAYER CAN RENEW YOUR
PASSION AND REDIRECT YOUR PATH

Date: _____

The way of the transgressor is hard, it is a path filled with empty promises, broken relationships, selfish decisions, guilt-ridden consequences and life-long regrets. It may promise pleasure, prosperity, and self-preservation, but the road of rebellion is a dead-end street, a cul-de-sac of despair.

Jonah had no idea how difficult travel would be when he paid the fare at Joppa and decided to go in the opposite direction of his ministry assignment. God instructed this contrary prophet to preach to the city of Nineveh and cry against its wickedness. The Lord, in His mercy, was willing to forgive the inhabitants of the Assyrian empire, but to do so, He needed a messenger of truth, a preacher to proclaim the way of the Lord.

Instead of complying to the commands of God, Jonah went in the opposite direction on a ship to Tarshish; when he faced a great storm, he jumped ship, and attempted to take his own life. Jonah, in his abounding sin, came face to face with abounding grace. God had prepared a great fish to swallow Jonah; for three days and three nights, he sank deep into the watery grave of the fish's belly. In utter misery, Jonah cried out to God for deliverance.

> "I went down to the bottoms of the mountains; the earth with her bars as about me forever: yet thou hast brought up my life from corruption, O LORD my God. When my soul fainted within me I remembered the LORD: and my prayer came in unto thee, into thine holy temple" (Jonah 2:6-7).

Instead of turning his eyes toward Nineveh (the place he was supposed to go), Jonah vowed to first turn his eyes toward the temple, the very presence of God. This was a crucial element of his prayer. With this vow, he showed true repentance. To get back on the right path, he not only needed to get to Nineveh, he needed to get to God. The good news: God allows U-turns!

Stuck in a whale, in the depths of the sea, Jonah literally had nowhere to go. In response to Jonah's repentance, the Lord caused the fish to "vomit out Jonah upon the dry land" (Jonah 2:10).

If Jonah had prayed with such tenacity of heart when God first called him, he could have avoided his hellish experience. But the truth is, Jonah's story is not necessarily about the misadventures of a sinful prophet; rather it is about the patience, the lovingkindness, and the forgiveness of a merciful God. The Lord not only restored the ministry of a stubborn preacher, but through the stubborn preacher, God redeemed the sins of a wicked nation, teaching us that prayer makes a clear path a path of righteousness for every individual who has ever found themselves on a dead-end street.

PRAYER PRINCIPLE

Prayer is the only pathway that leads to God after having traveled down the road of rebellion. In true repentance, when we pray, God will turn our lives around thus renewing our passion for Him.

PRAYER POINTS:

- Prayerlessness at the beginning of a ministry assignment may cause rebellion in the heart of the minister.
- The path of a prayerless saint leads to sinfulness.
- God is willing to allow someone to experience travail of soul in order to bring that individual back to Himself.
- Prayer can restore, renew, and redirect a man's life.

PRAYER PASSAGES

- "And the word of the LORD came unto Jonah the second time, saying, Arise, go unto Nineveh, that great city, and preach unto it the preaching that I bid thee" (Jonah 3:1).
- "He maketh me to lie down in green pastures: he leadeth me beside still waters. He restoreth my soul: he leadeth me in the paths of righteousness for his name's sake" (Psalm 23:2-3).

PRAYER PETITION

Wonderful, Merciful Savior, I seek Your face in my rebellion, I look to Your holy temple in my despair. My steps have taken me away from Your holy hill. Wash me, that I may be whiter than snow. Redirect my heart back to You and put my feet on righteous paths.

PRAYER PONDERINGS:

In what ways do you relate to Jonah?

_____

_____

_____

_____

_____

Why do you think Jonah ran away from his assignment?

_____

_____

_____

_____

_____

Read the 2nd chapter of Jonah and discuss the content of his prayer.

_____

_____

_____

_____

_____

What steps must be taken for the believer after reconciliation?

_____

_____

_____

_____

_____

PRAYER PAGE:

What I have learned today about prayer:

_____

_____

_____

_____

_____

Today I am thankful for:

_____

_____

_____

_____

Today I am asking for:

_____

_____

_____

_____

My confession before God today is:

_____

_____

_____

_____

"There has never been a spiritual awakening in any country or locality that did not begin in united prayer."

– A.T. Pierson

31

THE PRAYER OF

NEHEMIAH

HOW PRAYER CAN SPARK
THE FLAME OF NATIONAL REVIVAL

Date: _____

It was a scene of apocalyptic proportion. Ash and smoke filled the horizon and could be detected from miles away. The smoldering embers of what used to be the glorious gates of the city was a dreadful reminder of Israel's sin. The great and impregnable wall, now reduced to mountainous piles of rubble, gave witness to the broken lives of those who once lived within its borders. The holy temple of the Lord was reduced to nothing more than dust and debris. Vacant, void, and utterly vexed, the holy city of God was in ruins, and His people in captivity.

While in Shushan the palace, serving as a cupbearer for king Artaxerxes, Nehemiah received the news of Jerusalem's reproach. Upon hearing the report of his hometown, Nehemiah fell to the earth, wept bitterly, fasted for several days, and then did the only thing he was able to do...he prayed. Not only did Nehemiah pray, he repented, he mourned, he begged God for mercy. He did this not only for himself, but for his nation, his family, his people. He confessed his own sins before God and acknowledged the corruption that filled the hearts of those who broke the Lord's commandments. As the city of God burned with fire, the God of the city began fanning a flame in the heart of His servant.

Little did Nehemiah know that his prayer of repentance would be the spark of national revival. The burden of the cupbearer would grow stronger and deeper in the days ahead. Through the providence of God, Nehemiah was granted permission by Artaxerxes to rebuild the wall and repair the gates of Jerusalem. Though opposed on every side, the "good hand of God" was upon him. Astoundingly, the wall was rebuilt in only fifty-two days! The prayer of Nehemiah burned with passion until it blazed a revival spirit in the hearts of everyone around him.

National revival is always sparked by a solitary prayer. Be certain, it will take more than a single flame to consume the hearts of the people, but a single flame is all God needs to get started. How quickly the fire of prayer spreads when blown by holy whisper. God builds His kingdom on the backs of praying people. Every great stirring, every great revival, every great move of God in history can be traced back to a solitary, supplicating saint.

What consolation, what promise, what hope there is for us in this truth. Our world lies in sinful waste, our society in moral ruin, our churches in spiritual despair. But suppose we prayed? I mean really prayed. It could very well be that within your petition God has placed something flammable, something that would cause others, possibly the entire nation, to burn with holy desire.

PRAYER PRINCIPLE

God can ignite the flames of revival through the prayers of those who earnestly seek Him. When a man or woman becomes burden for the spiritual condition of those around him, God will prompt their hearts, through prayer, to do something about it.

PRAYER POINTS:

- Whenever God decides to work among His people, He always does so in accordance with prayer.
- Sincerity, intensity, and brokenness are the components of revival praying.
- Prayer is the means of national and global change.
- Only God can spread the fiery prayer from saint to saint.

PRAYER PASSAGES

- "Then the king said unto me, For what dost thou make request? So I prayed to the God of heaven" (Nehemiah 2:4).
- "Nevertheless we made our prayer unto God, and set a watch against them day and night, because of them" (Nehemiah 4:9).

PRAYER PETITION

Heavenly Father, help me to see the spiritual condition of my heart, my home, my city, my state, my country, and my world. I repent of my sins and ask that You extend mercy to those around me. Restore Your glory in our midst and stir a revival spirit in our souls. In Your name, Amen.

PRAYER PONDERINGS:

Study Nehemiah and cite all the passages in which he prayed.

_____

_____

_____

_____

_____

Do you believe national revival is a possibility in these days?

_____

_____

_____

_____

_____

Do you make it a habit to pray with others on a regular basis?

_____

_____

_____

_____

_____

What is revival in your opinion? Do you truly want it or pray for it?

_____

_____

_____

_____

_____

PRAYER PAGE:

What I have learned today about prayer:

_____

_____

_____

_____

_____

Today I am thankful for:

_____

_____

_____

_____

_____

Today I am asking for:

_____

_____

_____

_____

_____

My confession before God today is:

_____

_____

_____

_____

_____

"To pray without expectation is to misunderstand the whole concept of prayer and relationship with God."

– A.W. Tozer

32

SIMEON & ANNA

HOW PRAYING WITH EXPECTATION
PROVIDES AN ANSWER FROM GOD

Date: _____

When we ask something of the Lord in prayer, it must be done so with a spirit of expectation. Faithless is the prayer, when offered, that has no anticipation of an answer. Jesus said, "Therefore I say unto you, What things soever ye desire, when ye pray, believe that ye receive them, and ye shall have them" (Mark 11:24). Receiving an answer to prayer is contingent upon believing that God can provide an answer when we ask in the spirit of faith. This is not wishful thinking; this is faith in action through prayer. Such faith is predicated upon the promises of God, and upon the very nature of the One Who bids us to ask. "The value of the promise," said Andrew Murray, "depends upon the promiser: it is on my knowledge of what the promiser is that in the promise depends."

Simeon and Anna were two senior saints who believed in the promises of God because they believed in the Promiser. They prayed with a spirit of expectation, a spirit of faith. They longed to see the Messiah of Israel; and God, by their prayer of faith, gave them an answer in measure to their asking. Simeon was a devout man, one who "waited for the consolation of Israel." Anna was a widow who tirelessly served in the temple with "fasting and prayers night and day." Both had prayed to see the face of Messiah before their deaths. When Mary and Joseph brought Jesus to the temple for his dedication, they received, after years of prayer, their answer. Having seen the face of the Messiah, Simeon worshipped:

> "Then he took him up in his arms, and blessed God, and said, Lord, now lettest thou thy servant depart in peace, according to thy word: For mine eyes have seen thy salvation" (Luke 2:28-30)

Likewise, Anna rejoiced:

> "And she coming in that instant gave thanks likewise unto the Lord, and spake of him in all that looked for redemption in Jerusalem" (Luke 2:38).

For years they patiently waited for God to provide an answer. They trusted that He would bring to pass that which they had requested. They believed, therefore, they received. Andrew Murray is helpful once again in his remarks:

> "Faith is the confidence with which we persevere in prayer. It may only be later that you shall have it in personal experience; but now, without seeing, you are to believe that is has been given you of the Father in heaven."

God will never refuse the petition of those who ask with a spirit of faith, for it is in the believing that God works His very promises.

PRAYER PRINCIPLE

God provides an answer to prayer, not just in the asking, but in the believing. When we substantiate our faith on the One who has promised, we can fully anticipate that the promise will be fulfilled.

PRAYER POINTS:

- Praying in faith will always be in line with His promises.
- When we pray, we should fully expect God to bring to pass that which we have believed.
- When God prolongs an answer, it gives more opportunity to anticipate His response.
- Answers to prayer are designed to bring glory to the One Who provided the answer.

PRAYER PASSAGES

- "And all things, whatsoever ye shall ask in prayer, believing, ye shall receive" (Matthew 21:22)
- "If any of you lack wisdom, let him ask of God, that giveth to all men liberally, and upbraideth not; and it shall be given him. But let him ask in faith, nothing wavering. For he that wavereth is like a wave of the sea driven with the wind and tossed" (James 1:5-6).

PRAYER PETITION

Holy God, Give me faith, not only to ask for what I should, but to believe with a spirit of expectation. Help me to rely upon Your promises though the answer be prolonged. In Your name, I believe to receive.

PRAYER PONDERINGS:

If you could ask God for anything, what would it be?

_____

_____

_____

_____

_____

Do you believe God gives us "anything" we ask for? Explain.

_____

_____

_____

_____

_____

Is there anything you have been praying about for a long time?

_____

_____

_____

_____

_____

Does God provide answers to prayers when our faith is weak?

_____

_____

_____

_____

_____

PRAYER PAGE:

What I have learned today about prayer:

_____
_____
_____
_____
_____

Today I am thankful for:

_____
_____
_____
_____
_____

Today I am asking for:

_____
_____
_____
_____
_____

My confession before God today is:

_____
_____
_____
_____
_____

"How wonderful a means is prayer. The cry of a worm enters the ears of the Lord of Sabaoth, and He sends deliverance."

— William Plumer

33

THE PRAYER OF

MARY

HOW PRAYER PROMPTS THE SONG
OF SALVATION WITHIN THE BELIEVER

Date: _____

All throughout the Old Testament, we have an understanding of salvation as being faith in God. Repeatedly, we are told "the just shall live by faith." All the heroes in Hebrews eleven lived their lives by faith in God and it was counted unto them as righteousness. We find, however, in the pregnancy of Mary, an understanding of salvation that was somewhat concealed in the old covenant. Mary, having been overshadowed by the Holy Ghost, bore in her virgin womb the Son of the Highest, the Lamb of God.

Here, we see, for the first time in history, a greater revelation of true conversion. The Old Testament saints taught us that salvation meant having faith in God. Mary, pregnant with Christ, reveals that salvation is not only faith in God, but God *in* you *by* faith.

Imagine such a thing, the very God of glory abiding, dwelling, living in His own creation. Christ conceived in us is such an inconceivable thought that one can barely attempt to explain it.

And for Mary, explanations would be for another time and season. The mother of Jesus became so overwhelmed with the reality of God living in her that she burst out in worship and praise. In her prayer petition, known as the Magnificat, Mary expressed, with great gladness of heart, her redemption song. For Christ had not only come, He had come to deliver her from sin!

Mary's prayer praise was birthed from the reality of this glorious verse, "To whom God would make known what is the riches of the glory of this mystery among the Gentiles; which is Christ in you, the hope of glory" (Colossians 1:26). Christ in you! What an unforeseen truth, what an incredible thought, what a magnanimous consolation! God resides not in buildings made by human hand. He needs no temple, no tabernacle, no religious dwelling to make His abode. His desire is to occupy those whom He came to redeem.

Mary teaches us a proper response to such divine revelation. Overwhelmed with such blessed thought, she prayed with a heart of worship and magnified God as her Savior. Not only did her Redeemer live, He lived within her.

Nothing is more rapturous in prayer than when we realize that Christ dwells in our hearts by faith. What hope of glory there is in knowing that we are in Christ and Christ is in us, and Christ is in the Father.

Born anew in us is this Christ of heaven. Such holy thought, when impregnated into our soul, elicits the highest order of praise. God has given all His children a song of redemption. Nothing compels us to sing it more than when we realize Christ lives in us.

PRAYER PRINCIPLE

Every believer should approach their time in prayer with an understanding that Jesus Christ lives in their heart. Such a thought is the greatest motivation for sincere and genuine worship.

PRAYER POINTS:

- Salvation is not only faith in God but God in you by faith.
- Those who understand the reality of the abiding Christ will find their prayer lives to be filled with worship.
- When we have difficulty praying, we should always remember the truth that "Christ in us" is our hope of glory.
- The song of redemption should be sung with a heart of worship during our time of prayer.

PRAYER PASSAGES

- "But Mary kept all these things, and pondered them in her heart" (Luke 2:19).
- "God sent forth his Son, made of a woman, made under the law, To redeem them that were under the law, that we might receive the adoption of sons. And because ye are sons, God hath sent forth the Spirit of his Son into your hearts, crying, Abba, Father" (Galatians 4:5-6)

PRAYER PETITION

Holy Savior, What glorious thought it is that You live in me. You are the Vine and I am the branch; my life, my sustenance, my hope is found in You, and how wonderful it is to know that You are found in me.

PRAYER PONDERINGS:

Read Luke 1:46-56 and discuss Mary's prayer of praise.

_____

_____

_____

_____

_____

When you pray, do you consider the fact that Christ lives in you?

_____

_____

_____

_____

_____

Mary said that her soul magnified the Lord. How is this done?

_____

_____

_____

_____

_____

Explain salvation in terms of Christ being our hope of glory.

_____

_____

_____

_____

_____

PRAYER PAGE:

What I have learned today about prayer:

_____
_____
_____
_____
_____

Today I am thankful for:

_____
_____
_____
_____
_____

Today I am asking for:

_____
_____
_____
_____
_____

My confession before God today is:

_____
_____
_____
_____
_____

"Prayer as it comes from the saint is weak and languid; but when the arrow of a saint's prayer is put into the bow of Christ's intercession it pierces the throne of grace."

– Thomas Watson

34

THE PRAYER OF

PETER

HOW PRAYER PREPARES AND
EMPOWERS A BELIEVER FOR MINISTRY

Date: _____

For three years, Christ taught His disciples in the school of prayer. Every miracle, every sermon, every healing, every situation was a prayer lesson for the men whom He would entrust with the gospel. At the head of the class was Peter. As a student, he could be indifferent and ostentatious at times, but the Lord saw something in this "little rock" of a man. Not only was Peter head of the class, he was an integral part of Christ's inner prayer circle.

He saw up close and personal the power of prayer in His Savior. From the healing of his mother-in-law, to the prayer offered in the feeding of the multitudes, Peter got to experience what prophets, priests, and patriarchs had longed to hear: The prayers of the Messiah. Peter heard Him pray in the private moments of solitude. Peter saw the glory of God in prayer on the mount of transfiguration. He got to experience the suffering of Christ's prayer in the garden of Gethsemane. Daily, in all circumstances,

Peter was being taught the significance of prayer by the greatest prayer Teacher the world has ever known. But it was in Peter's biggest failure that he learned the most valuable lesson of prayer. For when he had denied the Lord three times, he remembered these incredible words, "But I have prayed for thee, that thy faith fail not: and when thou art converted, strengthen thy brethren" (Luke 22:32).

Little did Peter know that Christ's priestly prayer would be the flame that would ignite his own praying. It was in his weakest moment that he came to depend upon prayer as the source of his strength, as the power of his ministry.

After the ascension of Christ, we find Peter, along with the other disciples, praying for the promise of the Holy Spirit. With great power, he preached on the day of Pentecost to the saving of thousands. It was Peter, along with John, who went to the temple to pray; and in the spirit of prayer, healed the lame man who sat at the Beautiful Gate. After being beaten and imprisoned for the preaching of the resurrection, it was Peter who led the church in prayer for more boldness and courage. On the rooftop during a time of prayer, it was Peter who saw the vision of the great white sheet, which ultimately confirmed the salvation of the Gentiles. It was Peter, who through the power of prayer, fed the sheep of Christ's pasture, preached the gospel, and ministered to the saints.

What lesson there is for any student enrolled in the school of supplication. Our ability to serve, to lead, to preach, to witness, to fulfill any assignment, hinges upon our willingness to pray.

PRAYER PRINCIPLE

Prayer gives way to spiritual power in the work of the Lord. Without prayer, a believer may find himself impotent, indifferent, and disconnected with God; but through prayer, the work of the ministry is made possible because the minister is made strong.

PRAYER POINTS:

- The greatest example of prayer is given to us through the life and the teachings of Christ.
- Knowing that Christ prays for us should motivate us to pray to Christ.
- God empowers the saint who commits himself to prayer.
- The work of the ministry cannot be fulfilled apart from an ongoing and ceaseless prayer life.

PRAYER PASSAGES

- "And they continued steadfastly in the apostles' doctrine and fellowship, and in breaking of bread, and in prayers" (Acts 2:42)
- "Peter therefore was kept in prison: but prayer was made without ceasing of the church unto God for him" (Acts 12:5).

PRAYER PETITION

Awesome and Mighty God, The work of the ministry is too great for me to accomplish in the energy of my flesh. I ask You to empower me, enable me through the ministry of prayer to do all that You have called me to do.

PRAYER PONDERINGS:

How do you become a better student in the school of prayer?

_____

_____

_____

_____

_____

Have you ever felt the intercessory power of Christ in your failures?

_____

_____

_____

_____

_____

How does prayer specifically empower someone for the ministry?

_____

_____

_____

_____

_____

Review the book of Acts and discuss the accounts of Peter's prayers.

_____

_____

_____

_____

_____

PRAYER PAGE:

What I have learned today about prayer:

_____
_____
_____
_____
_____

Today I am thankful for:

_____
_____
_____
_____

Today I am asking for:

_____
_____
_____
_____

My confession before God today is:

_____
_____
_____
_____

"He that hears without ears understands us without our words. Yet as language is of absolute necessity in social prayer, that others may join us in our address to God, so for the most part we find it necessary in secret, too, for there are few persons of so steady and fixed a power of meditation as to maintain warm devotion and converse with God, or with themselves profitably, without words."

– Isaac Watts

35

THE PRAYER OF

JOHN

HOW LOVE FOR CHRIST
PROVIDES INTIMACY IN PRAYER

Date: _____

In the final hours of Jesus' life, we find John the Beloved drawing closer and closer to the side of Christ. The mood was somber, the revelations were shocking, and the hearts of the disciples were troubled as they realized this would be the last meal together with their Savior. Betrayal was among them and Christ was about to reveal the imposter. The heaviness of the moment seemed to press John into Jesus,

> "Now there was leaning on Jesus' bosom one of his disciples, whom Jesus loved. He then lying on Jesus' breast saith unto him, Lord, who is it?" (John 13:23,25)

As the other disciples began debating among themselves, John found his place in the lap of the Lord. So close was this beloved saint to Jesus that he could feel the holy breath of God upon his brow. And from that sacred side, he learned what true prayer is all about: Intimacy and fellowship with Christ.

More than any other New Testament writer, John teaches us, from his own experience, that prayer is not merely an exchange of words; prayer, by virtue of the relationship it represents, is the act of dwelling, abiding, and being with God through intimate fellowship. As a branch in the Vine, so observed John, we are to gain our sustenance, draw our strength, and produce our fruit from the abiding presence of Christ.

John teaches us that prayer, in short, is simply being close to God through our relationship with Jesus. P.T. Forsyth said, "The reality of prayer is bound up with the reality and intimacy of life. And its great object is to get home to God as Jesus is, and to win response even when we get no compliance." This is what prayer meant to John, simply leaning upon the bosom of heaven's Lamb. And the more intense life becomes, the greater the need to move closer to Him. So close to Him, that the very answer to prayer is Christ Himself. Through that holy union, the Lord gave John these wonderful truths about prayer:

> "If we confess our sins, he is faithful and just to forgive us our sins, and to cleanse us from all unrighteousness" (1 John 1:9)
> "And whatsoever we ask, we receive of him, because we keep his commandments, and do those things that are pleasing in his sight" (1 John 3:22)
> "And this is the confidence that we have in him, that, if we ask anything according to his will, he heareth us" (1 John 5:14)

Such divine revelation of prayer came through a life wholly committed to the very subject. When drawing close to His side we discover prayer's greatest purpose: Simply being with Jesus.

PRAYER PRINCIPLE

Prayer is more than an exchange of words; prayer is drawing close to the presence of God out of a sheer love and desire to be with Him in an intimate setting of fellowship.

PRAYER POINTS:

- Maintaining communion with Christ is a vital aspect of prayer, especially during moments of uncertainty.
- True fellowship begins with a love for Christ.
- We are in Christ, as a branch is in the Vine, not just to produce fruit, but to enjoy His presence.
- The greatest answer to prayer is being with Jesus.

PRAYER PASSAGES

- "That they all may be one; as thou, Father, art in me, and I in thee, that they also may be one in us: that the world may believe that thou has sent me" (John 17:21).
- "That which we have seen and heard declare we unto you, that ye may also have fellowship with us: and truly our fellowship is with the Father, and with his Son Jesus Christ" (1 John 1:3)

PRAYER PETITION

Holy Savior, Draw me close to Your side. Give me the joy of Your fellowship. Help me to see that in the most heated moments of life, I need to be close to You, learning of You, hearing Your words, and abiding in Your presence. Give me grace to draw near, and grace to stay still.

PRAYER PONDERINGS:

On a scale from 1 to 10, how close are you to the Lord?

_____

_____

_____

_____

_____

Do you sense His presence in your life when you pray?

_____

_____

_____

_____

_____

During troubled times, do you feel yourself pressing into Him?

_____

_____

_____

_____

_____

From John 15, explain how a believer produces fruit in his life.

_____

_____

_____

_____

_____

PRAYER PAGE:

What I have learned today about prayer:

_____

_____

_____

_____

_____

Today I am thankful for:

_____

_____

_____

_____

Today I am asking for:

_____

_____

_____

_____

My confession before God today is:

_____

_____

_____

_____

"Prayer must carry on our work as much as preaching; he preacheth not heartily to his people that will not pray for them."

– Richard Baxter

36

THE PRAYER OF

STEPHEN

HOW GOD USES PRAYER TO
CHANGE THE HEARTS OF SINNERS

Date: _____

With no financial backing, educational programs, marketing techniques, or large facilities, the early church in the book of Acts multiplied in number and increased in spiritual power. Heavy persecution caused the disciples to leave Jerusalem and proclaim Christ in the surrounding areas. The growth of Christianity was so rapid that the disciples recognized the need for organizational structure. Servant-deacons were appointed to help with the daily ministration of the widows so that the apostles could give themselves to prayer and preaching.

One of those servant-deacons was a man by the name of Stephen, who "full of faith and power, did great wonders and miracles among the people" (Acts 6:8). Not only did he have great organizational skills, he was also a powerful preacher of the gospel. So powerful was he at communicating the message of Christ, that certain leaders of the synagogue rose against him, accusing him of blasphemy against the law of Moses. As Stephen stood to defend himself, he began preaching against Israel's indifference to God. With sharp rebuke and convicting power, the Spirit of God "cut these men to the heart." In fury, they "cried with a loud voice, and stopped their ears, and ran upon him with one accord." With hatred in their hearts and large stones in their hands, they lay hold of Stephen and began publicly stoning him. Just before his death, he kneeled to the ground and amazingly began to pray, "Lord, lay not this sin to their charge." (Acts 7:60).

In the spirit of Christ's dying words, he interceded on their behalf and "fell asleep." The blood-stained ground where Stephen's body lay, would become the soil of gospel harvest. For in the background of that dreaded event, was a man by the name of Saul, who was consenting unto Stephen's death.

God answered Stephen's dying prayer just a few chapters later in the conversion of Saul of Tarsus. Though he hated the church and despised the name of Jesus, Saul could not escape the calloused murder of Stephen and the remarkable prayer he prayed.

Stephen's prayer reveals that God has the power to provide an answer even after we are gone. It was Stephen's final prayer, maybe more so than his fiery preaching, that captivated the attention of Saul's sinful heart. So powerful is prayer that it not only makes a dying man intercede for his enemies, but it makes his enemies become as the dying man. That is why it is vitally important to pray for our lost loved ones until our dying day. Many souls have been converted to Christ through the death of those they loved...and even those they hated.

PRAYER PRINCIPLE

Through prayer, God can change the hearts of sinners. Though we may never see the conversion of those we love, we have assurance that God can answer our prayers for their salvation even after we are gone.

PRAYER POINTS:

- To pray for the conversion of sinners is to pray like Christ.
- The work of the Holy Spirit through the power of prayer, has the ability to change people.
- God can answer our prayers even after our death.
- The fruit of prayer is greater and more abundant than we can ever imagine.

PRAYER PASSAGES

- "Then said Jesus, Father, forgive them; for they know not what they do. And they parted his raiment, and cast lots" (Luke 23:34).
- "And they stoned Stephen, calling upon God, and saying, Lord Jesus, receive my spirit" (Acts 7:59)

PRAYER PETITION

Merciful God, I intercede for the lost loved ones in my life. For my friends, my family, my neighbors, and my community, I beg You to spare their lives from judgment. Furthermore, I pray for my enemies. Grant them mercy to believe upon the name of Christ for salvation. Impart to them the knowledge of Jesus so that they might be spared from wrath.

PRAYER PONDERINGS:

How could Stephen pray such a merciful prayer?

_____

_____

_____

_____

_____

Do you pray for lost loved ones regularly? Who are they?

_____

_____

_____

_____

_____

Do you believe God answers our prayers even after we die?

_____

_____

_____

_____

_____

Discuss the fruit of Stephen's prayer as it relates to Paul's ministry.

_____

_____

_____

_____

_____

PRAYER PAGE:

What I have learned today about prayer:

_____
_____
_____
_____
_____

Today I am thankful for:

_____
_____
_____
_____
_____

Today I am asking for:

_____
_____
_____
_____
_____

My confession before God today is:

_____
_____
_____
_____
_____

"God will either give you
what you ask for, or something far better."
– Robert Murray McCheyne

37

THE PRAYER OF

CORNELIUS

HOW PRAYER OPENS THE
DOOR TO THE REVELATION OF GOD

Date: _____

Ironic is the activity of prayer in that so often we do not know what to pray for until we begin praying; and in the praying, God reveals by the Spirit the very thing we should be praying over. True prayer begins when we ask God for the thing He bids us to ask for. Only in the act of praying will God show us how and what to pray. In his book, *Quiet Talks on Prayer*, S.D. Gordon said,

> "Prayer needs an ear, a tongue, and an eye. First an ear to hear what God says, then a tongue to speak it, then an eye to look out for the results. The purpose of God comes in through the ear, passes through the heart taking on the tinge of the personality, and goes out at the tongue as prayer."

How often I have gone into the prayer closet with a set agenda, a list of items, and a resolved heart only to have God show me a better way to pray. God always gives light to the man sitting in darkness who truly longs for illumination.

Cornelius was such a man. He was a devout, God-fearing centurion who had a reputation of generosity in his Caesarean community. He, along with his family, were known to be people of prayer. Though he lived his life as an unconverted Gentile, he desired to know truth and sought earnestly to receive it.

God heard his prayers and through a series of providential events, brought the apostle Peter to the home of Cornelius. As a Jew, Peter was reluctant to enter the home of a Gentile; however, through the prompting of God, he began to preach the gospel of Jesus Christ. The Holy Spirit fell on them and in that moment Cornelius and his home were saved and baptized.

This historic event confirmed to the church at large that God was "no respecter of persons, but in every nation he that feareth him, and worketh righteousness, is accepted with him" (Acts 10:35). Those Jewish apostles were amazed because it solidified the truth that God's plan of salvation was for all men, Jew *and* Gentile, bond *and* free.

The conversion of Cornelius not only teaches us something about salvation; it teaches us something about supplication. When a man, through prayer, seeks to know the will of God, the mind of God, and the ways of God, God will illuminate his heart to the realities of truth. God taught Cornelius how to pray and what to pray for. Though he was an unconverted Gentile centurion, God enlightened him to salvation because that is what he sought after.

When a man searches, God shines a light. When he is hungry, God provides bread. When he is knocking, God opens the door. And when he truly prays, it'll be God showing him how to do it.

PRAYER PRINCIPLE

When an individual seeks to know the truth, God will disclose to that person a measure of revelation. Effectual, sincere, and honest praying begets illumination. When a man pursues the will of God, the God of that man's will *will* enlighten his soul.

PRAYER POINTS:

- The Spirit of God helps us in the asking of prayer.
- We pray as we ought only when God helps us to pray as we should.
- A man who desires the light of truth and pursues truth in prayer, will be positioned to receive what he desires.
- The work of God in prayer facilitates divine purposes that extend far beyond our own lives.

PRAYER PASSAGES

- "Likewise the Spirit also helpeth our infirmities: for we know not what we should pray for as we ought: but the Spirit itself maketh intercession for us with groanings which cannot be uttered" (Romans 8:26).
- "Ye ask and receive not, because ye ask amiss, that ye may consume it upon your own lusts" (James 4:3)

PRAYER PETITION

Heavenly Father, Give me ears to hear what You say, and a tongue to ask what You reveal, and eyes to see it come to pass by faith. Show me how I should pray and what I should pray for.

PRAYER PONDERINGS:

What factors are involved with hearing from God in prayer?

_____

_____

_____

_____

_____

How does the Holy Spirit help us when we pray?

_____

_____

_____

_____

_____

Can you recall a time when the Lord helped you pray? About what?

_____

_____

_____

_____

_____

Does God hear the prayer of the unsaved? Why or why not?

_____

_____

_____

_____

_____

PRAYER PAGE:

What I have learned today about prayer:

_____
_____
_____
_____
_____

Today I am thankful for:

_____
_____
_____
_____
_____

Today I am asking for:

_____
_____
_____
_____
_____

My confession before God today is:

_____
_____
_____
_____
_____

"Because the Church is God's beloved,
the care of it should be most in our mind, and the
love of the preservation of it should draw forth our
prayer most in favor of it."
– David Dickson

38

THE PRAYER OF

EPAPHRAS

HOW GOD BLESSES HIS CHURCH
THROUGH FERVENT PRAYER WARRIORS

Date: _____

Among the prominent and influential personalities in the New Testament, one rarely considers the name Epaphras. There are not many songs or sermons throughout church history that detail his life or ministry. As a matter of fact, he is only mentioned three times in the New Testament, twice in Colossians and once in Philemon. However, what we gather from those three references proves that Epaphras made a huge impact in his local church (Colossians 1:7, 4:12, Philemon 1:23):

- He was a member of the Colossian congregation.
- He was a dear servant among the people.
- He was a faith minister of Christ.
- He labored alongside the apostle Paul.
- He was with Paul, at some point, in prison.

During Paul's Roman imprisonment, the church of Colossae sent Epaphras to visit the apostle. Under the inspiration of the Holy

Spirit, Paul wrote the epistle to the Colossians and sent the letter back to the congregation in the hands of Epaphras. In that epistle, Paul said of this dear man:

> "Epaphras, who is one of you, a servant of Christ, saluteth you, always laboring fervently for you in prayers, that ye may stand perfect and complete in all the will of God" (Colossians 4:12).

Epaphras may have never built a church, started a mission, wrote an epistle, led a choir, taught a class, or preached a sermon, but he prayed for those who did. Such is the heartbeat of greatness in God's kingdom. Paul said that he "labored fervently" in prayer for the Colossians. The implication is that he worked intensely, he travailed earnestly, he put the sweat into it. With much pathos and passion, he pleaded with God for his fellow parishioners. He specifically prayed for them to not only know the will of God, but for them to know it and to stand perfectly in it.

If a local church is going to operate in the unction of the Spirit, it will require men like Epaphras to be on its membership roll. Blessed indeed is the assembly who has the gifted preachers, and the articulate teachers, and the skilled administrators, and the melodious singers, but the real power comes from the prayer warriors. God's abiding presence, His holy anointing, His heavenly favor shines upon the crowd who have men and women laboring in their prayer closets actively interceding for others.

Epaphras shows us that the greatest position in the church is the one on your knees in prayer for others.

PRAYER PRINCIPLE

The power of God is manifested in a local church through the faithful ministry of those who labor in prayer. Such individuals are content to be in the background knowing that God imparts unction in the secret places of prayer.

PRAYER POINTS:

- Not everyone with spiritual influence holds a title.
- Those who labor fervently in prayer help facilitate the work of the ministry in the church.
- The greatest prayer we can pray for anyone is for them to know the will of God and to stand perfectly in it.
- God blesses a congregation through the power of prayer.

PRAYER PASSAGES

- "I have set watchmen upon thy walls, O Jerusalem, which shall never hold their peace day nor night: ye that make mention of the LORD, keep not silence" (Isaiah 62:6).
- "For this cause we also, since the day we heard of it, do not cease to pray for you, and to desire that ye might be filled with the knowledge of his will in all wisdom and spiritual understanding" (Colossians 1:9)

PRAYER PETITION

Gracious and Almighty Father, I thank You for those men and women who labor fervently in prayer. They have refreshed my spirit, encouraged my walk, and interceded on my behalf. Help me to be labor with them.

PRAYER PONDERINGS:

Who comes to your mind when think of the term "prayer warrior"?

_____

_____

_____

_____

_____

How does prayer empower the church to function properly?

_____

_____

_____

_____

_____

Do you consider yourself to be an "Epaphras" to your congregation?

_____

_____

_____

_____

_____

What does it mean to "labor fervently" in prayer?

_____

_____

_____

_____

_____

PRAYER PAGE:

What I have learned today about prayer:

_____
_____
_____
_____
_____

Today I am thankful for:

_____
_____
_____
_____
_____

Today I am asking for:

_____
_____
_____
_____
_____

My confession before God today is:

_____
_____
_____
_____
_____

*"I have now concentrated all my prayers
into one, and that prayer is this, that I may die
to self, and live wholly to Him."*
— Charles Spurgeon

39

THE PRAYER OF

PAUL

HOW PRAYER IS THE ALL-CONSUMING
POWER OF LIFE AND MINISTRY

Date: _____

If prayer is the source of spiritual power, then it is easy to understand how the apostle Paul was the strongest Christian in the history of the church. From the onset of his conversion we find him waiting for Ananias in the house of Judas on the street called Straight; the Bible says of him, "behold, he prayeth" (Acts 9:11). This posture of prayer is one he would assume throughout the course of his life and ministry. Outside of Jesus Christ, we have no greater example, no greater teacher of prayer than Paul.

Most of what we know about prayer comes from his teachings. Paul instructs us to pray without ceasing, to pray one for another, to pray with thanksgiving, to pray with the armor of God, to pray in the Spirit, to pray for those in authority, to pray for all things in all situations. Down through the ages, his meticulous instruction on prayer has enabled the church to fulfill its assignment, proclaim its message, equip its followers, overcome its temptations, fight its enemy, and lovingly adore its Savior. The weight and authority of his teaching came from a life that was fully immersed, fully engaged in the practice of prayer. Paul was a great *instructor* of prayer because he was a great *intercessor* of prayer.

His epistles were not just letters to the various churches he established, they were prayer petitions written and offered to God through the leadership of the Holy Spirit. One only needs to read through the third chapter of Ephesians, the first chapter of Colossians, or the first chapter of 2 Thessalonians to discover Paul's intensity, passion, and fervency in prayer. Whether he was bound in prison, teaching in the synagogue, or traveling on his missionary journeys, he operated in the full force of prayer. E.M. Bounds said of Paul,

> "If Paul was the first of the apostles, prayer conspired to that end. He made praying a habit, a business, and a life. Praying made up the substance, the bone, the marrow, and the very being of his religious life."

His life was a ceaseless, unending, resolute, voluntary outpouring prayer to God. In his final testimony, he declared, "For I am now ready to be offered and the time of my departure is at hand" (2 Timothy 4:6). When the entirety of a man's life is given to prayer, he will see death as a final and rewarding answer to his lifelong request. This was Paul's crown of achievement...to enter into the presence of the One he had been praying to throughout the course of his ministry. History knows of Paul's power because heaven knew of his petitions. Such is the power of prayer. Everything is done by it, nothing without it.

PRAYER PRINCIPLE

There is no substitute for prayer in the work of the Lord. In order to build a life of ministry, we must be willing to build a life of prayer. Our ability to teach, preach, and serve others in the church resides in our willingness, our hunger even, to pray.

PRAYER POINTS:

- Prayer sets the trajectory and course of ministry.
- Only those who give themselves to prayer can spiritually influence and lead others in a godly manner.
- Ceaseless praying is made possible when we have an ever-abiding consciousness of the reality of God.
- Prayer is not just something we do; it is something we are.

PRAYER PASSAGES

- "For what thanks can we render to God again for you, for all the joy wherewith we joy for your sakes before our God; Night and day praying exceedingly that we might see your face, and might perfect that which is lacking in your faith?" (1 Thessalonians 3:9-10).
- "I will therefore that men pray ever where, lifting up holy hands, without wrath and doubting" (1 Timothy 2:8).

PRAYER PETITION

Heavenly Father, I ask that You make all my life a continual and perpetual prayer. May the longing of my soul, the power of my ministry, and the joy of my life to be in the uninterrupted presence of my King.

PRAYER PONDERINGS:

How did prayer set Paul apart from the other apostles?

_____

_____

_____

_____

_____

Read through any epistle of Paul and record his mention of prayer:

_____

_____

_____

_____

_____

List three ways in which one can engage in ceaseless prayer:

_____

_____

_____

_____

_____

Do you think you will be remembered as a man or woman of prayer?

_____

_____

_____

_____

_____

PRAYER PAGE:

What I have learned today about prayer:

_____

_____

_____

_____

_____

Today I am thankful for:

_____

_____

_____

_____

Today I am asking for:

_____

_____

_____

_____

My confession before God today is:

_____

_____

_____

_____

"Who is he that condemneth? It is Christ that died, yea rather, that is risen again, who is even at the right hand of God, who also maketh intercession for us."

– The Apostle Paul, Romans 8:34

40

THE PRAYER OF

JESUS

HOW PRAYER IS MADE POSSIBLE
THROUGH THE FINISHED WORK OF GOD'S SON

Date: _____

It would be easier to measure the weight and volume of all the oceans in the world than to describe the prayer life of the Son of God. No patriarch in history, no prophet in Israel, no priest in the temple has ever known in prayer what Christ *had* and eternally *has* with the Father. So sacred is this divine prayer union that only the Son can offer it, only the Spirit can communicate it, and only the Father can receive it. All that Jesus did during His earthly life was accomplished through the will of His Father as revealed to Him through prayer. At all times and in all situations, Jesus exemplified the life of prayer as the greatest example of prayer ever given.

We find Him praying in His temptation, at His baptism, and for His disciples. He prayed in public gatherings, on religious holy days, and in private settings. He can be found praying over meals, over the diseased, over His family, and over His nation. Prayer was His practice early in the morning, during the daytime, late in the evening, and many times throughout the night. Jesus prayed for Himself, by Himself, and in Himself. He prayed for people who loved Him and people who hated Him, for people living and for people not yet born. He taught on prayer, gave instruction on prayer, and lived out prayer before His disciples. He prayed in the upper room, in the Garden of Gethsemane, and on the cross of Calvary. His dying words are recorded in history as the final prayer petition to the Father on behalf of unrighteous sinners. His life was a continual, uninterrupted dialogue with the Father; and it is to this truth we discover the grandest reality of all: The prayer life of Jesus Christ makes our praying to God a possibility. In Christ, we find all that Adam lost in his garden prayers.

The death, burial, resurrection, and ascension of Jesus Christ positions and postures Him as our great High Priest, One Who "ever liveth to make intercession" (Hebrews 7:25). How blessedly eternal are His prayers for us. His life before the Father at the throne, is one of ceaseless supplication.

Therefore, when we pray to the Father through the name of Jesus Christ, He is joining us, nay, we are joining Him in the grand and glorious petitions made around the throne. We can "come boldly unto the throne of grace" because there in that holy place is the magnanimous Mediator, the providential Petitioner, the sovereign Supplicator praying for us, praying with us, and praying in us through the power of the Spirit of God who "maketh intercession for us with groanings which cannot be uttered" (Romans 8:26). Of all the benefits and blessings of Christ's prayer, none is greater than to be able to say, "Our Father" and to know that the Father, through His Son, hears and replies.

PRAYER PRINCIPLE:

The privilege of prayer, given to all believers, is made possible through the finished work of Christ. As our High Priest, He sits upon His throne continually making prayer a reality for us.

PRAYER POINTS:

- Adam lost fellowship with the Father through sin; Christ restored fellowship with the Father through sacrifice.
- Christ lived a life of prayer as the ultimate and divine example for all who follow Him.
- Through the Spirit of God, Christ prays for us with ongoing groanings that cannot be uttered.
- We can rightly and boldly call God our Father through the life and prayer of Jesus Christ.

PRAYER PASSAGES:

- "Then said Jesus, Father forgive them; for they know not what they do. And they parted his raiment, and cast lots" (Luke 23:34).
- "Wherefore, holy brethren, partakers of the heavenly calling, consider the Apostle and High Priest of our profession, Christ Jesus;" (Hebrews 3:1).

PRAYER PETITION:

Great and Holy God, My prayers are only made possible through Your prayers. You have and You always will be praying for me. Upon Your authority, and by Your power I call You my Father which art in heaven!

PRAYER PONDERINGS:

Citing Scripture, how is your prayer heard by the heavenly Father?

_____

_____

_____

_____

_____

According to Hebrews 4:16, what should be our attitude in prayer?

_____

_____

_____

_____

_____

Discuss how Jesus employed prayers during His times of difficulty.

_____

_____

_____

_____

_____

Describe your relationship with God right now through Christ.

_____

_____

_____

_____

_____

PRAYER PAGE:

What I have learned today about prayer:

_____

_____

_____

_____

_____

Today I am thankful for:

_____

_____

_____

_____

_____

Today I am asking for:

_____

_____

_____

_____

_____

My confession before God today is:

_____

_____

_____

_____

_____

GOD AROSE

So oft opposed, when ere I go,
to God in prayer by subtle foe.

I do suppose, the devil knows,
before the Lord my faith will grow.

And so he sows, down here below,
the seeds of doubt in every row.

But in the woe, with mighty bow,
the Lord is strong, and overthrows.

And so it goes, in prayer I show,
that Satan ran when God arose!

HEAVEN'S PRAYER

I stand before the Holy King,
endowed with glory to adore.
In royal form, His scepter brings,
The answer now forevermore.

I bow before the Holy Lamb,
enshrined with honor, strength, and love.
What scars that mark the Great I AM,
and tell the story of His blood!

I come before the Holy Priest,
endued with power to perform.
Beyond the veil His mercy brings,
my soul to God in quick reform.

I walk before the Shepherd Great,
enriched to lay in pastures green.
Though shadows all but be my fate,
His rod and staff now comfort me.

I fall before my Holy God,
enjoined with others to declare.
Eternal praise on heaven's sod,
My prayer will have no amen there.

ALL OF ME

My treasure brought for all to see, unto the Lord on bended knee.

No pleasure found; how can this be?

Tis not the **gift** He wants, but me.

With prose so grand I call to Thee; in eloquence I make my plea.

Opposed, the Holy Spirit grieves,

Tis not the **words** He wants, but me.

Like Abraham I give my seed, the altar bound so righteously.

But in the ram God meets my need,

Tis not the **child** He wants, but me.

With tune and tone in symphony, a splendid voice I sing with ease.

Yet heaven holds no harmony,

Tis not the **song** He wants, but me.

Before the throne, each moment flees, at length I groan to which I plea.

The clock I watch so patiently,

Tis not the **time** He wants, but me.

With nothing left I now agree, a broken heart is all he needs.

My soul contrite, contend to be,

Before the Lord is **all of me.**

THE HOLY SPIRIT GROANS

When I believed myself alone,
with stammering words toward Thy throne;
there is no praise or hymn or song,
but then the Holy Spirit groans.

I try to sing but verse is gone,
I try to think but thoughts are wrong;
I try to pray but merely moan,
and then the Holy Spirit groans.

How is it that my heart is known?
How is it that my soul is sown?
How does my prayer make heaven's home?
Alas, the Holy Spirit groans.

With sacred hush His joy is shown,
into my soul, into my bone;
The dross within my heart is drown,
Thank God the Holy Spirit groans.

THE HINDER PART

There is a cleft within my heart,
of which I long to stand.

To catch a glimpse of glory sought,
to holy comprehend.

And though I cannot fully know
the sum of all He is,

Tis my request the hinder part,
of which I can't dismiss.

AGAIN, I PRAY!

The heavens stay, the famine sore,
the barren field, the hunger more.
I lift my head, the rain delays,
with longing heart, again I pray!

I look for dew at morning's dawn,
but find no trace, where it belongs.
So, like the hart, which runs away,
in thirst for God, again I pray!

The bearing sun, a cloudless sky,
a famished plea, a frantic cry.
Does heaven know, all that I say?
Regardless still, again I pray!

Alas I hear, a distant sound,
the echoes of a thunderous pound.
The promise of my God awaits,
with eager soul, again I pray!

The dusty soil, no longer more,
the flood has come, the water pours,
into my soul, His flowing grace,
with thankful heart, again I pray!

DRAWING NIGH

No greater pursuit can ere be found,
than drawing my soul to Thy holy ground.

I cast off my shoes and stand in the midst,
Near Thy flaming fire, I cannot resist.

To turn and behold this wonderful sight,
the glory of God outshines the noon light.

And just like the bush that glows with such pow'r,
The same is my heart in prayer at that hour.

BIBLIOGRAPHY

Alexander, Eric. *Prayer: A Biblical Perspective.* Carlisle, Pennsylvania: The Banner of Truth Trust, 2013.

An Unknown Christian. *The Kneeling Christian.* Public domain.

Bounds, E.M. *The Power of Prayer.* Grand Rapids, MI: Zondervan, 1955.

Bounds, E.M. *The Purpose in Prayer.* Chicago, IL: Moody Press, 1968.

Bounds, E.M. *The Complete Works of E.M. Bounds.* Grand Rapids, MI: Baker Books, 1990.

Brase, Lee. Praying from God's Heart. Colorado Springs, CO: NavPress, 1993.

Brooks, Thomas. *Smooth Stones taken from Ancient Brooks.* Carlisle, Pennsylvania: The Banner of Truth Trust, 2011.

Brooks, Thomas. *The Secret Key to Heaven.* Carlisle, Pennsylvania: The Banner of Truth Trust, 2006.

Brother Lawrence. *The Practice and Presence of God.* Grand Rapid, MI: Spire Publishing, 1967.

Bunyan, John. *Prayer.* Carlisle, Pennsylvania: The Banner of Truth Trust, 2020.

Carson, D.A. *Praying with Paul: A Call to Spiritual Formation.* Grand Rapids, MI: Baker Academics, 2014.

Chadwick, Samuel. *The Path of Prayer*. Fort Washington, PA: CLC Publications, 2000.

Duewel, Wesley. *Mighty Prevailing Prayer*. Grand Rapids, MI: Zondervan Publishing House, 1990.

Duewel, Wesley. *Touch the World Through Prayer*. Grand Rapids, MI: Zondervan Publishing House, 1986.

Edwards, Jonathan. *The Life and Diary of David Brainerd*. Public domain.

Gordon, S.D. *Quiet Talks on Prayer*. Shippensburg, PA: Mercy Place Publishing, 2003.

Hallesby, Ole. *Prayer*. Minneapolis, MN: Augsburg Publishing House, 1994.

Law, William. *A Serious Call to a Devout and Holy Life*. Public domain.

Lawson, James Gilchrist. *Deeper Experiences of Famous Christians*. Anderson, IN: Warner Press, 1981.

McIntyre, David. *The Hidden Life of Prayer*. Public domain.

Moody, D.L. *Prevailing Prayer*. Public domain.

Mueller, George. *Answers to Prayer*. Public domain.

Murray, Andrew. *With Christ in the School of Prayer*. Public domain.

Owen, John. *Communion with God*. Carlisle, Pennsylvania: The Banner of Truth Trust, 2016.

Owen, John. *The Glory of Christ*. Carlisle, Pennsylvania: The Banner of Truth Trust, 2018.

Ravenhill, Leonard. *Why Revival Tarries.* Minneapolis, MN: Bethany Fellowship, Inc., 1979.

Ryle, J.C. *A Call to Prayer.* Carlisle, Pennsylvania: The Banner of Truth Trust, 2020.

Spurgeon, Charles. *Morning by Morning.* Public domain.

Spurgeon, Charles. *The Pastor in Prayer.* Greenville, SC: Emerald House Group, 2001.

Torrey, R.A. *How to Pray.* New Kensington, PA: Whitaker House Publishing, 1983.

Torrey, R.A. *The Power of Prayer.* Grand Rapids, MI: Zondervan Publishing House, 1955.

Tozer, A.W. *Paths to Power.* Harrisburg, PA: Christian Publications, Inc., Date Not Included.

Tozer, A.W. *Prayer.* Chicago, IL: Moody Press, 2016.

Watts, Isaac. *A Guide to Prayer.* Carlisle, Pennsylvania: The Banner of Truth Trust, 2019.

Wells, Albert M. *Inspiring Quotations.* Nashville, TN: Thomas Nelson Publishers, 1988.

Whitney, Donald. *Praying the Bible.* Wheaton, IL: Crossway, 2015.

Whitney, Donald S. *Spiritual Disciplines for the Christian Life.* Colorado Springs, CO: NavPress, 1991.

Yancey, Philip. *Prayer: Does It Make Any Difference.* Grand Rapids, MI: Zondervan Publishing, 2009.

ABOUT THE AUTHOR

Kenneth Kuykendall has been the pastor of Cross Roads Baptist Church in Lawrenceville, Georgia since 2008. Under his leadership, the church has experienced spiritual growth, numerical increase, and facility expansion for years. His burden for ministry is to equip the saints, reach the unsaved with the gospel, and glorify Christ through expositional preaching and teaching.

In addition to the pastorate, he has written many books and Christian literature for ministry. In 2007, he started *Cross Roads Publications* which provides a variety of resources for churches, ministers, and individuals. He is also the founder of *Seeds for the Soul Daily Devotion*, a devotional ministry that reaches hundreds of thousands of subscribers.

He enjoys reading, praying, writing, hiking, running, and spending time with his family. He and his wife Heather have been married since 2000. They, along with their three sons, Brady, Drew, and Carson currently live in Loganville, GA.

Other Devotional Titles by the Author

Thrive

Pull Up a Seat

A Collection of Seasons

In and Out of Season

Somewhere in the Shadows

Meditations for Ministry

The Joy of Devotion

Just Like Jesus

order online at crossroadspublications.org